FOOD 2.0

FOOD 2.0
CHARLIE AYERS
WITH KAREN ALEXANDER AND CAROLYN HUMPHRIES

London, New York, Melbourne, Munich, and Delhi

Project Manager and Editor: Norma MacMillan
Project Art Editors and Designers: Smith & Gilmour, London
Photographer: Noel Murphy

Senior Editor (US): Shannon Beatty
Editor (US): Christy Lusiak
Production Editor: Jenny Woodcock
Production Controller: Sarah Sherlock

First American edition, 2008

Published in the United States by
DK Publishing, 375 Hudson Street, New York, New York 10014

08 4 6 8 10 9 7 5 3 1

BD527—May 2008

Published in Great Britain by Dorling Kindersley Limited.

A catalog record for this book is available from the Library of Congress

ISBN 978-0-7566-3358-5

DK books are available at special discounts for bulk purchases for sales
promotions, premiums, fund-raising, or educational use. For details, contact:
DK Publishing Special Markets, 375 Hudson Street, New York, NY 10014.
SpecialSales@DK.com

Printed and bound in China by Sheck Wah Tong Printing Press Ltd.

Discover more at **www.dk.com**

CONTENTS

WELCOME TO FOOD 2.0

SMART CHOICES

THE SMART PANTRY

SMART RECIPES

WELCOME TO FOOD 2.0

// I WAS HIRED TO FEED GOOGLE INC. BACK IN NOVEMBER 1999, WHEN THE COMPANY WAS YOUNG AND SMALL, AND HUNGRY FOR PROGRESS. CO-FOUNDERS LARRY PAGE AND SERGEY BRIN WERE LOOKING TO PROVIDE THEIR EMPLOYEES WITH FAST, UNFETTERED ACCESS TO CLEAN, HEALTHY, DELICIOUS FOODS. THEIR GOAL WAS TO NOURISH THE BODIES AND BRAINS AND SPIRITS THAT WOULD PROPEL THEIR FAST-GROWING COMPANY FORWARD. THEY WANTED POWER FOODS THAT WOULD LEAVE THEIR MINIONS STIMULATED AND ENERGETIC AFTER LUNCH, NOT SLUMPED OVER THEIR KEYBOARDS. AND THEY WANTED IT DONE WITH THE HIGHEST QUALITY ORGANIC, SUSTAINABLE-SOURCED INGREDIENTS IN AN ENVIRONMENT THAT MADE THEIR BRAINY, ECLECTIC EMPLOYEES FEEL LIKE A FAMILY.

// I was employee number 53 at Google, and even though I really wanted the job I thought Larry and Sergey were crazy when they hired me. Sergey told me that Google would grow to be tens of thousands of employees. I laughed and said, "Some of the best restaurants in Palo Alto are all around you. Go there." Sergey said that was not very efficient—it takes away from their productivity to have everyone going out to eat. Those Google guys (in the beginning, they really were all guys) were curious and adventurous, and wanted exciting flavors. They were from all parts of the country, and all over the world. They were young, most of them recently out of school, and they worked all the time. They missed their families and they missed their mamas' cooking. They were eating burritos and pizza every day because they barely had time to shower, much less worry about what to eat.

// When I left Google in May 2005, I had five sous chefs and 150 employees working for me in 10 cafés across the company's sprawling Mountain View, California, headquarters. We were serving 4,000 lunches and dinners daily to a team of people as diverse and hard-working as any on the planet. I learned so much from my family of clients at Google. Inspired by their sense of adventure, and blessed with the incredible bounty of clean, sustainable, amazing foods available here in California, I came to believe that we can all eat delicious, clean, fast cuisine that is good for us, good for the community, and good for the Earth. I want to help people eat better, and if we don't have a lot of time, then let's do it quickly.

I WANT TO HELP PEOPLE EAT BETTER.

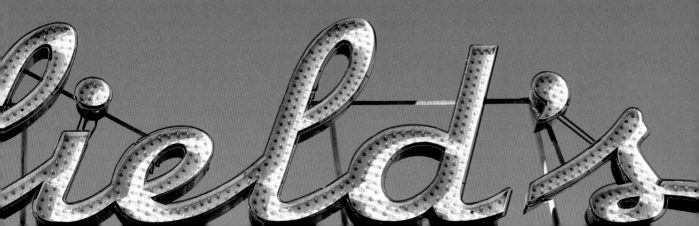

Charleston Rd ➔
← Garcia Ave

YOU'RE SMART. SO WHY DON'T YOU EAT THAT WAY?

// I BELIEVE THIS GENERATION HAS SUCH AN OPPORTUNITY TO EAT WELL AND DO IT THE RIGHT WAY, BUT MOST OF THE TIME WE'RE JUST BLOWING IT. PEOPLE ALWAYS THINK, WELL, I HAVE TO EAT SOMETHING QUICKLY SO IT HAS TO BE BAD FOR ME. MY ANSWER TO THAT IS, WHY?

// Each snack and each meal you eat is an opportunity to make a difference—in your body and your world. At Google, Sergey and Larry believed that if everyone were eating healthy and eating well, they were going to have healthy, productive, happy, and efficient engineers working for them. It made sense for them as a business investment, even if there were cheaper alternatives available, and it makes sense for you, too. Invest in yourself. Make smart choices, eat great food, and reap the dividends.

EACH MEAL IS AN OPPORTUNITY TO MAKE A DIFFERENCE—IN YOUR BODY AND YOUR WORLD.

FAST, RAW, AND ORGANIC.

THAT'S WHAT I'M THINKING WHEN I COOK

// Fast. Food does not need to be unhealthy to be prepared quickly. Some of the healthiest, most delicious foods are straight out of nature and don't take any time to prepare.

// Raw. You don't have to eat raw at every meal. After all, this is a cook book! But raw food is great for you, and despite my years of experience as a chef, I continue to find that often the best thing you can do to a good piece of food is to leave it alone.

// Organic. Be intelligent about your food. Organic, clean, sustainable-farmed food is imperative. But not all organic food is equal. If something is imported from far away, or comes swathed in too much packaging, it's not clean at all. It has probably done more harm than good to the environment—your environment—en route to your mouth.

GO ORGANIC

// JUST BECAUSE THERE'S AN "ORGANIC" STICKER ON MY APPLE DOESN'T MEAN IT'S ALWAYS THE BEST CHOICE. I BELIEVE WHOLEHEARTEDLY IN CHOOSING ORGANIC PRODUCTS WHEN THEY'RE AVAILABLE LOCALLY, BUT GIVEN THE CHOICE BETWEEN AN ORGANICALLY GROWN APPLE THAT CAME OFF A CARGO JET FROM CHILE AND A PIECE OF IN-SEASON FRUIT THAT WAS GROWN NEARBY WITHOUT PESTICIDES, I'LL CHOOSE THE LOCAL FOOD ANY DAY.

// Getting smart about your food involves taking a little extra time to consider the impact of what you're eating—on yourself and on your environment. It means investing a few extra minutes with the shopping cart or the restaurant menu to learn more about what you're buying. Once you get into the rhythm of shopping that way and you become familiar with the best local food sources available in your area, it really doesn't take much time at all.

// There's a lot of highly processed junk food in the supermarket made with organic ingredients. And a lot of otherwise clean, wholesome products come wrapped in an obscene amount of nonrenewable packaging that will be jamming the landfills for decades to come. Just because a sandwich cookie is organic doesn't mean you should eat it.

THERE'S A LOT OF HIGHLY PROCESSED JUNK FOOD MADE WITH ORGANIC INGREDIENTS.

3 QUICK RULES FOR HOW TO EAT

1 READ LABELS

2 ASK QUESTIONS

3 CONSIDER YOUR OWN VALUES

ORGANICS: WHY THE "BIG O" MATTERS

// Organics are not the only path to clean, smart food. But the Big O still reigns supreme. Organic, locally sourced food is the ideal. Why? Because most of the chemicals used on nonorganic foods are byproducts of petroleum, which is not a good ingredient for recipes. That's nasty, and I don't know how it's considered okay to feed people like that.

// Even food that is totally pesticide-free may have been grown with synthetic fertilizers that are unhealthy for the soil, the local environment, and you. Organic means the soil is clean, the water is clean, and your food is clean. It means you get less poison for your money.

// What's your inner voice saying to you? Does it matter, or doesn't it matter? You can take all the information that's presented to you and make a reasonable decision about whether the actions you're taking are going to have that big of an impact. Sometimes you might indulge in something a little naughty, but if you eat clean most of the time you won't feel so guilty when you slip up a little bit.

ORGANIC SIMPLY MEANS TRYING TO AVOID CRAP IN YOUR FOOD.

READ THE LABEL

// Check the label. If it doesn't sound like food, it probably isn't. The ingredients listed first are the ones that are most plentiful in a product. For example, in breads and cereals, you should always look for whole grains at the top of the list. Wheat flour is not a whole grain unless it says "Whole Wheat Flour."

LOOKING FOR THE PUREST FORM OF AN INGREDIENT IS THE BEST APPROACH

//

> For juices, this means making sure it says "not from concentrate."
> When shopping for beef, or dairy products from cows' milk, look for "grass fed."
> When purchasing eggs from chickens, ducks, quail, and geese, look for "pastured eggs."
> If you are buying oils, look for "cold-pressed" and "unrefined."
> Shopping for beer, wine, and alcohols, look for small batch distilleries, locally microbrewed beer, and boutique wineries.

//

IF IT DOESN'T SOUND LIKE FOOD, IT PROBABLY ISN'T.

STUFF TO AVOID FEEDING TO YOURSELF OR PEOPLE YOU LOVE:

PESTICIDES

HYDROGENATED OILS

CORN SYRUP

REFINED SUGARS

THE PRESERVATIVES SODIUM NITRATE AND SODIUM NITRITE

THINGS YOU CAN'T PRONOUNCE

BE NOSY

// The easiest way to make sure you're eating smart is to ask questions of the people who are selling you food—in the supermarket or the farm stand or the restaurant. Be nosy. Make friends with your local merchants and store owners. Build relationships with them so you're comfortable asking them questions and they're comfortable telling you the truth.

// I'm nosy. At restaurants, I stick my head in the kitchen to see what's going on. I've gone behind restaurants and looked in the garbage to see what they were using. This one guy said he wasn't using ketchup in his Korean barbecue sauce. I wanted to know what was in it, so I pulled up behind the place and I saw a big can of ketchup in his dumpster.

GOOD QUESTIONS TO ASK OF THE PEOPLE WHO SELL YOU FOOD
//
> Where was this grown or raised?
> Was it treated with pesticides?
> When did this shipment arrive?
> What's in season right now?
> Are you expecting any great deliveries that I shouldn't miss this week?
> Can you recommend something delicious to go with the fresh wild salmon I just bought?
//

AT RESTAURANTS, I STICK MY HEAD IN THE KITCHEN TO SEE WHAT'S GOING ON.

KEEP IT LOCAL

// I like to impose a 150-mile (240-kilometer) travel limit on my food as much as possible. If you buy food that has been grown or raised locally, it will be fresher, cheaper, and more delicious. It will have generated a lot less pollution and earth-warming greenhouse gases on the way to your mouth. What's more, buying local products will help sustain and nourish your local marketplace to ensure that bountiful fresh, local, clean food will continue to be available to you.

// Where I live, in the San Francisco Bay Area, you don't need to go farther than a 150-mile (240-kilometer) radius to get anything—except coffee beans, bananas, and the ingredients to make chocolate. We live in the midst of a wonderful cornucopia of bounty, from fish and meats and dairy to produce and wine. I can even buy local lemongrass and ginger now. Still, there are always going to be some things that by nature call for an exception to the rule, such as the exotic curry powders and spices and sauces I buy from various ethnic markets. Although you won't always be able to find what you're looking for locally, it pays to ask. Going to your local farmers' market is a tremendous way to learn about what your region has to offer.

FOOD GROWN OR RAISED LOCALLY WILL BE FRESHER, CHEAPER, AND MORE DELICIOUS.

APPRECIATE THE SOURCE

// One of my primary goals at Google was teaching people to appreciate how their food was produced. Because all of my delicious food was served free to Google employees, I wanted to make sure they were not taking it for granted. I wanted them to understand what kind of thought and resources had gone into growing it; I wanted to establish a connection between the land and the people who ate from it—even if they worked in cubicles and played roller hockey on an asphalt parking lot. If I could make smart eaters out of people, I could help make them into smart citizens and smart consumers, too.

// Often, we'd be lucky enough to discover a personal connection to a terrific crop of something special. Googlers loved food that had a story behind it, and when they knew it was from someone in their own society they were even more excited about it. That always reminded me how important it is to take the time to learn the stories behind our food. When we appreciate its source, we are enhancing our own ability to enjoy it and make the most of what we eat.

// One Googler's dad grew figs out in Modesto. One day I got to work and opened my big refrigerator to find six flats of gorgeous figs sitting there. I was baffled, until I got this email from him later in the day: "I brought you some figs." I called them "the prized Kamangar figs" after this guy, Salar Kamangar, and his dad who had grown them, and we celebrated them for a week at a time when they were in season.

TAKE THE TIME TO LEARN THE STORIES BEHIND YOUR FOOD.

EAT IT RAW!

// SOMETIMES, THE BEST WAY TO COOK FOOD IS NOT TO COOK IT AT ALL. RAW FOODS ARE ESSENTIAL TO PRESERVING AND FORTIFYING THE DIGESTIVE ENZYMES FOUND IN OUR BODIES, WHICH CAN BECOME DEPLETED AS WE AGE. NATURAL ENZYMES THAT OCCUR IN RAW FRUITS AND VEGETABLES ARE DESTROYED BY COOKING AND PROCESSING FOODS, WHICH IN TURN REQUIRES OUR BODIES TO USE UP MORE OF OUR VALUABLE ENZYMES DIGESTING THOSE FOODS. DIGESTIVE ENZYMES ARE ESSENTIAL FOR THE BODY TO PROPERLY UTILIZE NUTRIENTS AND VITAMINS, SO WHEN THEY ARE DEPLETED WE CAN EXPERIENCE A LACK OF ENERGY, OR EVEN DIGESTIVE PROBLEMS.

// At Google, where maintaining the diners' energy was a key goal of my cooking, I made sure to offer at least two raw salads every day. The ingredients received no heat whatsoever.

// Eating raw foods just makes me feel alive. I actually catch a buzz from eating sushi. And there's no better way to save time making a meal than to skip the cooking part altogether. Just be sure to always wash fruits and vegetables extra thoroughly before eating them raw, even the packaged ones like those "prewashed" bags of salad.

YOU CAN SAVE TIME AND ENZYMES BY EATING RAW FOODS.

5 EASY WAYS TO GO RAW

1 HAVE A SALAD

2 GRAB A PIECE OF FRUIT OR A BUNCH OF CHERRY TOMATOES TO SNACK ON

3 PUT AN EXTRA HANDFUL OF LIGHTLY DRESSED MACHE LETTUCE UNDER A PIECE OF GRILLED FISH

4 KEEP A BAG OF BABY CARROTS OPEN ON THE PASSENGER SEAT WHILE YOU DRIVE

5 DRINK A FRESH FRUIT SMOOTHIE FOR BREAKFAST

FRUIT. PLAN AHEAD

// Except for the occasional banana, no one would eat fresh fruit at Google unless I had peeled it and cut it up for them. Are we all really that lazy? Maybe we're just too busy to bother.

// Sadly, I'm not going to be there to cut your fruit for you every day, so you've got to think ahead and do it for yourself—before you're hungry.

HOW TO MAKE SURE YOU EAT FRUIT

//

> Keep a tub of cut pineapple, mango, papaya, berries, or melon in the refrigerator all the time.
> Apple slices will keep nicely in a bag in the refrigerator if you first toss them in water with a little bit of lemon juice added, then drain them and pat them dry.
> Strawberries and stone fruits (peaches, plums, apricots, and nectarines) get mushy if you cut them in advance. Wash them up good as soon as you get them home, and you'll be able to grab a mouthful of sweetness whenever you're feeling hungry.
> Whip up a quick smoothie or toss a couple of handfuls of fresh fruit into your yogurt in the morning.
> Layer pear or apple slices onto your sandwiches.
> Toss a handful of berries atop your salad.
> Make a fruit salad salsa (see opposite) to spoon on top of fish or poultry. I like to serve this salsa over my lobster tacos.

//

RECIPE // FRUIT SALAD SALSA

> Combine 3 cups seedless watermelon diced small (about ⅓ of a melon, depending on its size), 2 jalapeño peppers diced with seeds (or 1 serrano pepper), ¼ cup mint leaves cut into ribbons, ½ cup very roughly chopped cilantro leaves, 1 cup diced red onion, some lime juice to taste, and cracked black pepper. Add salt at the very last moment, because the salt draws out the liquid from the melon and makes a watery mess.

IT PAYS TO HAVE YOUR OWN JUICER. STORE-BOUGHT FRUIT JUICES ARE PASTEURIZED, AND THEY LOSE A LOT OF FLAVOR AND NUTRIENTS IN THE PROCESS.

VEGGIES. YOU CAN'T LIVE WITHOUT THEM

// Keep a crudité in your crisper at all times, ready to go—while you're listening to music, or waiting for your dinner to cook, just cut up a huge bag of vegetables. Make carrot and celery sticks, and jicama and cucumber spears. Wash up some cherry tomatoes. On a lazy day, all that and a bowl of hummus or guacamole can pass for a meal!

// One exception: Don't eat raw cauliflower or raw broccoli, because your body doesn't digest them well and you won't get the whole nutritional value out of them. But don't overcook them either. If you blanch them lightly, they'll keep that delicious crunch and the flavors will peak, too.

RECIPE // A GREAT SALAD TO KEEP IN THE FRIDGE

> Toss together some jicama, radishes, lime juice, and a little cayenne pepper. Then drop in some orange segments. In a salad I try to go for that sweet-salty-sour synergy and I want to be sure it's going to have some crunch to it. This one hits all those elements at once.

DRINK YOUR GREENS

// Wheatgrass is great for cleansing the blood of toxins. It also contains strong digestive properties, making it a good choice for those with slow digestion or constipation. If taken before a meal, wheatgrass helps you digest your meal properly and move it along through your system. If taken after a meal, your body is more likely to absorb its nutritional values.

// Now I'm a wheatgrass believer. The stuff just makes you feel alive. Good, fresh wheatgrass has a sweet finish to it, and you feel great after you drink it. I think the people at Google got into it because they saw that we were willing to be goofy with them to get them to try new things. I didn't mind putting on a show to get people to do something good for them. I recommend drinking wheatgrass straight up, not adding it to anything else.

// Some people do experience some unpleasant effects from drinking wheatgrass (such as diarrhea and headaches). If this happens more than a couple of times after you first start incorporating wheatgrass into your lifestyle, then you are either taking too much or it's simply not for you.

// I had never been a fan of wheatgrass before, but one of the cooks who worked for me at Google was this big surfer from Santa Cruz, and he loved it. He convinced me to offer wheatgrass shots in the vegetarian section of the café, and it took off like crazy. I had one woman who did nothing but trim wheatgrass, grind it up, and pour it into shot glasses. We even had a little bell you could ring after you downed a shot. Drinking this thing that was good for you just became part of the culture, and pretty soon we were grinding up 250 shots a day—20 flats of wheatgrass—and the bell was going off all the time.

RAW JUICE SNACKS

// Raw juice drinks will keep you feeling alive and pure—all the hippies in Northern California love them!

// If you purchase fruits and vegetables already manipulated, the prep time for these drinks will be far less than if you start with whole produce, but if you enjoy saving money, buy them in their entirety. To make things easy, use a high-quality vegetable juicer, something that can stand up to lots of abuse.

RECIPE // BEET-CARROT-GINGER FIZZ

> Juice 3 peeled carrots, 1 peeled large, fresh beet, and ½in (1cm) peeled piece of fresh ginger root. Pour over ice in a highball glass. Top off with sparkling water, stir, and sip through a straw.

RECIPE // CARROT-CUCUMBER LEMONADE

> Juice ⅓ peeled English cucumber and 3 peeled carrots. Mix with 2 tsp fresh lemon juice and chill. Drink this cold (no ice), garnished with a thin slice of cucumber.

RECIPE // CARROT-CELERY-APPLE JUICE

> Juice 2 peeled large carrots, 2 celery ribs, and 1 cored apple. Chill. Garnish with a small rib of celery, if you want, and drink cold (no ice).

RECIPE // CARROT-GINGER-ORANGE JUICE

> Juice 4 peeled carrots, 1in (2.5cm) peeled piece of fresh ginger root, and 2 peeled large oranges. Chill. Drink cold (no ice). This is good with vodka—it's the sassy cousin to Screwy Rabbit (see page 114).

RECIPE // CARROT-PARSLEY JUICE

> Juice a handful of fresh parsley, including the stems (I like the curly leaf for juicing and flat-leaf for cooking), and 4 peeled large carrots. Chill. Drink cold (no ice), garnished with a sprig of parsley.

RECIPE // SPICY TOMATO-CELERY-LIME

> Juice 1 peeled small lime, 1 small, fresh jalapeño chili (seeded or not, depending on how much fire you want), 2 large, ripe tomatoes, and 2 celery ribs. Pour over ice in a chunky glass and garnish with a slice of lime. You can add vodka for an evening reviver!

RECIPE // THREE-MELON CRUSH

> Juice ¼ each cantaloupe, honeydew, and Crenshaw melon (all peeled and roughly cut up). Pour over crushed ice in a large glass. Experiment with other combinations of melons, too.

RECIPE // PINEAPPLE-GRAPEFRUIT JUICE

> Thinly pare a strip of zest from 1 ruby red grapefruit and cut in thin strips. Peel the rest of the fruit. Juice the grapefruit and 1 small pineapple (peeled and sliced). Pour over crushed ice in a large glass and garnish with the grapefruit zest.

RAW FISH. BUY IT, CUT IT, EAT IT

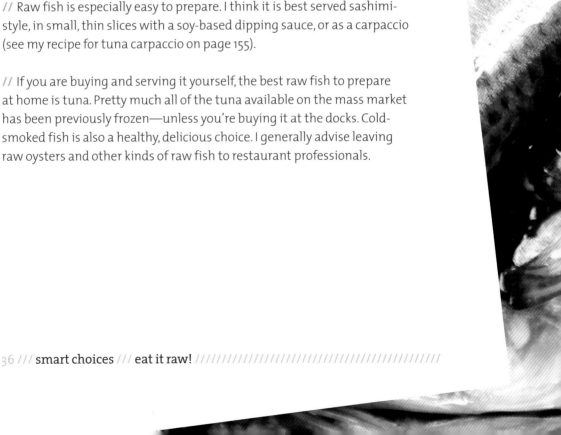

// Fish is brain food, period. I remember in the early days, before I started serving dinner at Google, Sergey would order up platters and platters of sushi from some local high end sushi joint. He often came downstairs to the café, where I was busy cleaning and preparing for the next day's lunch, to share some with me. I thought it was pretty nice of him to remember me down there.

// Maybe Sergey just loved sushi. Or maybe he loved sushi because he knew that fish is super high in Omega-3, which is a crucial fatty acid we need in our daily diets. The fat found in fish helps make the cell membranes found in the brain more elastic and more able to absorb nutrients easily, which aids in brain development early on in life and then helps maintain the ability to learn new things as we grow older. These fats help to create stems to other cells. As I see it, fish is a great source for this natural lube we need to keep our minds up and running, ready to receive and respond.

// Raw fish is especially easy to prepare. I think it is best served sashimi-style, in small, thin slices with a soy-based dipping sauce, or as a carpaccio (see my recipe for tuna carpaccio on page 155).

// If you are buying and serving it yourself, the best raw fish to prepare at home is tuna. Pretty much all of the tuna available on the mass market has been previously frozen—unless you're buying it at the docks. Cold-smoked fish is also a healthy, delicious choice. I generally advise leaving raw oysters and other kinds of raw fish to restaurant professionals.

HOW TO BUY THE FRESHEST TUNA TO EAT RAW

//

> If it's a whole fish, make sure the eyes are clear, not cloudy.
> Poke at the flesh. Does it spring back, or does your finger leave
an indentation? You want fish that springs back quickly.
> Look for tuna that is a bright, deep red. Avoid fish that is graying
or that has an oxidized rainbow look.
> Be sure to ask when and where it was caught, and when your
fish merchant received it.

//

FISH IS A GREAT SOURCE OF THE NATURAL LUBE WE NEED TO KEEP OUR MINDS UP AND RUNNING.

A FASCINATION WITH FERMENTATION

// ACROSS THE GLOBE, EATERS HAVE FIGURED OUT THAT FERMENTATION IS A GREAT WAY TO EAT. FROM PICKLED GINGER WITH SUSHI AND INDIAN PICKLED MANGO WITH CURRY TO DILL PICKLES WITH A PASTRAMI SANDWICH, FERMENTED FOODS ARE DELICIOUS. AND THEY CAN SERVE A VITAL PURPOSE IN PROTECTING YOUR HEALTH.

// There are plenty more fermented foods we eat on a daily basis that we all love and don't even realize they are fermented. Bread, yogurt, cheese, and even chocolate all undergo fermentation. And drinks? Tea, coffee, wine, and my choice—beer—are fermented, as is miso paste, a particular favorite of mine. At Google I made enormous vats of Korean kimchi (see the recipe below, given to me by my friend Nina Kim). Everybody loved it.

// A custodian of your gastrointestinal track, fermentation works to keep your insides clean by helping to fight off microorganisms in your food and giving you a healthy constitution, so to speak.

RECIPE // NINA'S KIMCHI

> Toss a large head of napa cabbage, cut in bite-size pieces, with 2 tbsp kosher salt, then drain in a colander for 3 hours. Rinse well, drain, and dry. Mix with 4 sliced green onions (scallions), a handful of chopped cilantro, 1 tbsp each black and white sesame seeds, ¼ cup rice vinegar, the juice of a lime, 1 tbsp toasted sesame oil, and 2 tbsp (or more) *sambal oelek* in a nonreactive bowl. Cover and let marinate at least overnight (it gets better over a week's time). This makes about 1 ½lb (675g).

YOUR PANTRY. A COOK'S DATABASE

// I'M A CONSTANTLY CURIOUS COOK, SO I'M ALWAYS WILLING TO TRY OUT NEW THINGS AND EXPERIMENT ON MYSELF FIRST. IF IT GOES WELL, I'LL TRY IT OUT ON OTHERS. I SHOP AT A LOT OF ETHNIC MARKETS BECAUSE THEY OFTEN HAVE REALLY GOOD DEALS AND I CAN FIND THINGS YOU WOULDN'T SEE ANYWHERE ELSE. WHEN I GET THE CHANCE TO VISIT A NEW STORE, I HEAD FOR THE SUNDRIES FIRST TO CHECK OUT WHAT KINDS OF VINEGARS AND OILS AND SALTS AND SPICES THEY HAVE. I'M ALWAYS EAGER TO FIND SOMETHING I'VE NEVER SEEN BEFORE.

// My wife, Kimmie, is really good about being willing to taste new things. I try to cook for my family as much as possible, and so they get to try out a lot of the weird stuff I find. My pantry is where most of my eclectic purchases end up. It's my cooking database, so to speak. I'll try something out, and even if it's not right I'll remember the flavors and try it again later on something else. I think a diverse and well-stocked pantry is the key to being a quick, versatile cook.

I FIND A LOT OF GREAT WEIRD STUFF IN ETHNIC MARKETS.

VINEGAR. THE UNSUNG HERO OF FLAVOR

// Good, tasty vinegar can be the crowning glory to your dish, a zesty shot of flavor that helps brighten all the other surrounding tastes. I have 20 or more vinegars in my pantry. It's one of my favorite things to buy, and I find that having several different vinegars on hand offers me a lot of flavor flexibility when I'm working on a new dish.

// When cooking meat or chicken, the sweeter, fruity vinegars are great for deglazing your pan to create a nice *au jus* sauce. I'll just add a little bit right to the hot pan juices and stir it up. No additional heat is necessary, and it will meld right in to create a delicious sauce. It reduces rapidly and has a great intense flavor. But don't add too much or your whole dish will taste like salad dressing.

VINEGAR NEEDS GREAT FLAVOR THAT WON'T OVERPOWER THE FOOD.

MY 4 FAVORITE VINEGAR PAIRINGS

1 APPLE CIDER VINEGAR
OR BALSAMIC-FIG VINEGAR WITH PORK

2 CHINESE BLACK VINEGAR WITH
STIR-FRIED BEEF

3 RICE VINEGAR WITH STEAMED
SEA BASS OR TUNA

4 UME PLUM VINEGAR WITH
ROASTED TURKEY LEG

TOP FAVORITE VINEGARS I USE MOST FREQUENTLY AT HOME

//

> **Chinese black vinegar**. I use this in the base of many different Asian or East Asian-influenced dishes.

> **Japanese ume plum vinegar**. It's wonderful in a cold composed salad made with fresh corn and barley.

> **Rice vinegar**. Makes a wonderful dipping sauce for tempura vegetables.

> **Red wine vinegar**. Perfect for your basic French vinaigrette with shallots and Dijon mustard.

> **White wine vinegar**. Chardonnay, Champagne, and Muscat are all good for deglazing and making quick pan sauces.

> **Banyuls vinegar**. This is a good finishing vinegar for that sweet and sour profile.

> **Apple cider vinegar**. Use it in pork brine or turkey brine recipes.

> **50-year-old aged balsamic vinegar**. Use it for finishing over grilled meats. Balsamic-fig vinegar is worth looking for.

> **Sherry vinegar**. Good for Spanish-influenced dishes, roasted mushrooms, game birds, and polenta.

> **Brown rice vinegar**. I use it in place of rice vinegar when I'm looking to add that crunchy hippie twist to a recipe.

> **Malt vinegar**. Duh. It goes on fish and chips.

//

RECIPE // VANILLA-INFUSED VINEGAR

> Score a vanilla bean several times, then lightly toast it in a nonstick pan, just until it becomes fragrant. Drop it into a bottle of high-quality, mild vinegar (apple cider vinegar works well; or you could use rice vinegar). Close tightly and let steep for 2 weeks. Then begin to explore its flavors.

VINAIGRETTES

// I love to make my own vinaigrettes. Your basic ratio for vinaigrette is one part vinegar to three parts oil. Sometimes I'll add a little bit of fruit juice that matches and pairs well with the particular flavor. It can help take the edge off your vinegar and keep it from tasting too intense.

// Depending on how fancy you want to get, you can always add some spices or ginger, garlic, or shallots to give your dressing extra depth. I like to toast cumin or coriander seeds and grind them fresh into a vinaigrette. Or, you can make a reduction using some shallots and ginger or garlic and a little fruit juice. When it's reduced by half, remove it from the heat and hit it with the vinegar, right in the pan. Let it cool, and whisk in the oil.

RECIPE // ORANGE-MISO VINAIGRETTE

> Mix 1 tbsp white miso paste, 1 cup fresh squeezed orange juice, 1 tbsp minced pickled ginger, 1 tsp mustard powder, 3 tbsp canola oil, and 1 tsp toasted sesame oil in a bar blender. Serve over roasted beets and arugula with crispy shallots, garnished with black and white sesame seeds. Seared ahi tuna served rare goes well with this.

RECIPE // LEMON-SHALLOT VINAIGRETTE

> Combine the juice from a lemon, 1 tsp Dijon mustard, ½ tsp red wine vinegar, and 1 tsp minced shallots in a bowl. Whisk in 4 tbsp extra virgin olive oil and add salt and pepper to taste. You can add any fresh herb— chives, thyme, tarragon, chervil—or add them all and make it a Green Goddess dressing.

RECIPE // WASABI VINAIGRETTE

> Throw 3 tbsp rice vinegar, 2 tbsp wasabi powder, 4 tbsp mayonnaise, ½ tsp each toasted sesame oil, lime juice, and tamari, 1 tsp black sesame seeds, and 1 ½ tbsp minced green onion (scallion) in a glass jar. Close the top and shake away. Serve this over slightly grilled endive and frisée, alongside pan-roasted salmon or shrimp.

SALTS

// Salts from different regions around the world often have very distinct flavors, textures, and smells, which can really work to enliven and authenticate the flavor of different ethnic cuisines. I love tasting the different minerals in salt and trying to imagine where they came from. The shades of pink and gray can be very beautiful.

// Remember to season your food inside and out for a consistent flavor all the way through. If you're cooking a chicken breast, you'll want to season the stuffing and the inside and outside of the chicken equally. Season the flour for coating, too. With salt and seasonings, you are creating layers of flavors. You are assigning your food a texture and a smell, and you usually want that to be consistent throughout the dish.

// But how much salt? I think too much is when you can taste salt before you can taste what it is that has been salted. Of course, if you are supposed to be watching your sodium intake for health reasons, don't cheat. Protect your health first, your flavors second, so you can keep cooking and eating good food for a long time to come.

WHEN TO LAY OFF THE SALT
//
> I avoid salting mushrooms while cooking them as this helps to give them a really nice color. If you salt your mushrooms in the pan, all the juices exude from them and you end up with a pan of mushroom liquid and poached mushrooms rather than pan-roasted or sautéed.
> I don't put salt in a marinade.
> Never add salt to the water you are cooking your beans in.
> Salt tends to make root vegetables too mushy, because the pores in the vegetable tighten when cooking in salted water. If you cook your root vegetables in unsalted water, you're allowing them to take in the water and cook evenly from the inside out, rather than the other way around.
//

OILS. NOT JUST FOR COOKING

// Oils can go rancid pretty quickly in the pantry. If you don't use them often, you might consider storing them in the refrigerator if there's space. If you do refrigerate your oil, you will need to leave a little extra time for it to return to room temperature before you pour it.

THESE ARE MY FAVORITE OILS

//

> **Olive oil**. I use high-quality extra virgin olive oil only for finishing a dish, or in a vinaigrette. For cooking purposes, save your money and use regular olive oil, or canola or grapeseed oil.

> **Citrus oils**. I keep several different kinds of concentrated citrus oils, which I use to add a bright shot of flavor without having to drag out the citrus juicer. They are great for raw marinades, and for layering in flavor at the end of cooking. A very small amount goes a long way. Try adding a splash of orange oil to your vinaigrette to serve with Belgian endive or watercress salads, or add a drop or two of lemon oil to marinades for lamb or fish.

> **Rice-bran oil**. I've recently been turned on to this oil, which is great because it has absolutely no flavor. It's good for infused oils or vinaigrettes, when you want to taste everything else, but not the oil.

> **Toasted sesame oil**. I only use sesame oil in very small amounts. It smells good, but I find it can easily overpower the food.

//

CHEESE-FLAVORED OILS

// I make my own deliciously flavored oils by infusing them with cheese rinds. Olive oils infused with Spanish Manchego cheese or Parmesan are two of my favorites. Make the oils in small quantities. If you're not going to use them up quickly, they should be refrigerated. After six months or so, you need to start all over with a fresh sterile bottle and add new cheese rinds and flavorings to fresh oil.

RECIPE // MANCHEGO OR PARMESAN OIL

> Stuff cheese rinds saved from Manchego or Parmesan cheese into a sterilized wine bottle and add a couple of cracked black peppercorns, coriander seeds, fennel pollen (which you can order online), and bay leaves. Or add strips of orange or lemon rind instead—it depends on the flavor you're looking for. Pour in olive oil. Cork the bottle back up and let it sit for several days before using.

GREAT WAYS TO USE CHEESE-FLAVORED OIL

///

> Dress organic baby arugula leaves and roasted beets—unbeatable with Parmesan cheese oil—and season with a small amount of kosher salt and freshly ground black pepper.
> Toss in at the end of a pasta dish.
> Drizzle over steamed fish.
> Use as a dipping oil for fresh bread.

///

THE GRAIN GAME

MY FAVORITE GRAINS

//

> **Millet**. This is bird food to everyone else, but I love it. Boil it up and add it to soups or stews, or to vegetarian chili, about an hour before the dish has finished cooking. It blossoms nicely to fill out the dish, making it more substantial and satisfying.

> **Corn meal**. White for grits, yellow for polenta.

> **Farro**. Also known as emmer, this ancient strain of wheat is far more durable than its cousin durum, which is more commonly consumed around the world. Farro is widely eaten in Umbria and Tuscany in Italy— the über pastamaker will tell you that wheat flour derived from farro is the best to use when it comes to pastamaking. Look for it in specialist grocery stores and online.

> **Quinoa**. Great in soups, stuffing, and salads, and it makes a nice pilaf. Even better, quinoa is the only grain that is also complete protein. Always rinse quinoa thoroughly before you cook it or else it will have an offensive odor after it cooks.

> **Kamut**. I like kamut cold in a salad with dried fruits, fruit juices, cinnamon, and ginger. It's one of my favorite combinations.

> **Barley**. Even though pearl barley doesn't have a whole hell of a lot of nutritional value, it adds real body and substance to a lot of dishes. Used sparingly, I think barley is silky and satisfying.

//

RECIPE // CHEESE GRITS

> Put 2 cups each milk and water (or all water for a less creamy finish) in a heavy-based pan with 1 tsp kosher salt and some black pepper and bring to a boil. Gradually whisk in 1 cup stoneground white grits. Turn the heat to low, cover, and cook, stirring occasionally, until thick, about 15 minutes. Stir in 1 cup shredded sharp Cheddar cheese and 1–2 tbsp butter, plus some Google hot sauce (see page 249) or other hot sauce, if liked. Serves 4

NUTS AND SEEDS

KEEP THESE FOR MIXING INTO COOKING OR SALADS, AND FOR GENERAL MUNCHING

///

> Almonds
> Pistachios
> Toasted hemp seeds
> Sunflower seeds
> Pine nuts
> Cashews
> Black and white sesame seeds

///

FLAX SEED

> We all know flax seed is super healthy for you, but it has to be toasted and worked carefully into a dish or it will taste gritty—and you walk around with what looks like sand in your teeth all day. I use flax seed mostly in muffins and pancakes.

IT'S TRUE THAT NUTS AND SEEDS ARE HIGH IN FAT, BUT IT'S MOSTLY THE HEALTHY TYPE.

EAT YOUR BEANS

// I've always appreciated the flavor and texture of beans. There's something calming and relaxing and settling about a good dish of beans. While there are producers of good organic canned beans, I tend to favor the texture of dried beans in my cooking when there's time.

// You have to remember to soak dried beans overnight or they won't be ready to go when it's time to cook. Even letting them soak all day while you're at work is usually good enough. But if you forget, you can cheat. All you have to do is boil the beans quickly in a pot of water, then cover them, remove from the heat, and let them soak for about an hour. Drain away the liquid and you're ready to go.

// When it comes to cooking the beans, it's a good idea to boil rapidly for the first 10 minutes to remove any toxins before reducing the heat to simmer them until they are tender.

NEVER ADD SALT TO YOUR BEANS WHEN THEY'RE COOKING. IT HARDENS THEM UP AND THEY NEVER FULLY COOK.

BLACK BEANS
KIDNEY BEANS
SPLIT PEAS

I EAT CARBS

// Have you noticed that everyone who was on the Atkins diet is now off it? Carbs—pasta, bread, and rice—are back. In particular, pasta is a quick, fast-cooking food that yields high returns. I just try not to abuse it and eat it too much. My advice is, be smart. If you're eating pasta, don't also eat bread with your meal.

// I keep a lot of different kinds of rice around. Brown rice is nutty, slightly chewy, and aromatic—just amazing all on its own when fresh from the rice cooker. I'm also a big fan of the parboiled basmati rice that I buy from an Indian supermarket near me. Parboiled rice takes less time to prepare, and it cooks up more evenly.

MY TIPS FOR COOKING AND EATING PASTA

//

> I use really salty water to boil my pastas. You don't want just a sprinkle of salt. You want it to be noticeable in your water so the pasta absorbs that salty flavor.

> You can make a really good, really fast pasta tossed with canned tuna fish, canned tomatoes, capers, and lemon.

> I buy sealed packages of fresh lo mein noodles from the refrigerator section at the Asian supermarket. They're addictive. I cook them up spicy with garlic and chili paste, and end up eating the whole pan of noodles.

> You're free to experiment with whole wheat pasta. No doubt it's better for you, but I've tried it and I just can't find one I like.

//

COOKING RICE

> People often cook rice too quickly. If it is really boiling rapidly, the water evaporates too soon and your grains end up mushy. You want to go for a slow, long boil. A good rice cooker makes that easy. You might have to play around with it a little to get the right amount of liquid for each kind of rice, but once you figure this out a rice cooker really does the job nicely.

TURN UP THE HEAT

// If you like spicy food, as I do, you'll appreciate a wide variety of hot sauces in your pantry. I have friends from cooking school who make some crazy hot sauces that you have to sign a waiver just to buy. I'm not that nuts, but I do like having the option of turning up the heat when I cook.

// At Google, hot food—like a lot of other things—became a kind of geeky macho thing. It was their rite of passage, so they just sucked up my hot sauce. It's so hot you wouldn't want to eat it straight. I use it as a base for other things. It was a tremendous recipe that started with 6 quarts of habaneros, 2 quarts of jalapeños, and 14 dried chipotles. Do not worry. I've scaled it down for you (see the recipe on page 249).

// I'll use ready-made hot sauces in my recipes, primarily to save time—and so I'm not burning up my eyes mincing chilies all the time. I really like Sriracha Hot Chili Sauce, a Vietnamese-style product that comes in a squeeze bottle with a rooster on it. You can find it at most Asian markets or order it online. At Google, we used so much of this chili sauce that we referred to it as "special red sauce #2." Special red sauce #1 was ketchup.

// This Google guy Dan O'Brien gave me a batch of chilies in 2002, which his dad had grown in New Mexico. One little flake was like fire. I had this whole big bag full of them, and now they're almost gone.

CHILI-HOT VINEGAR

// You can use chili peppers to make your own spicy vinegars, which you can use like Tabasco sauce. I was on a spicy chicken wing kick for a while, and for them I made some great, fiery vinegar using about three dozen packets of chili flakes that I had left over from the pizza delivery guy! This made a huge batch of vinegar, but you can do it with a much smaller amount of chili flakes (the amount you use depends on the level of pain you can endure, and the type of chili flakes).

// Here's the trick: I put some of my batch into a squirt bottle. As the chicken wings came out of the oven, I deglazed them right in the pan with my chili vinegar. The vinegar melded beautifully with the pan juices to make a perfect spicy chicken wing sauce.

// But a stern safety warning: Keep your head far away from your oven-hot pan when you are dousing it with your homemade pepper spray. When that vinegar hits the heat, it steams up into a sizzling cloud of tear gas. You don't want your eyes or nose anywhere near that situation. I learned that the hard way.

RECIPE // CHILI-INFUSED VINEGAR

> Toast about 1 tbsp chili flakes in a pan, then grind them up in a coffee grinder. (A very important note: Only do this if you keep a separate grinder for spices. Otherwise, your coffee will forever taste like pepper spray.) Funnel the powder into 1 ½ cups of vinegar, add 1 tsp salt, and let it sit.

RECIPE // HOT CHICKEN WINGS

> Heat a sauté pan, then toss in the desired amount of wings plus some salt and pepper and a small amount of ketchup or hot chili sauce. Give the wings a good coating, to get some color on them, then roast at 400°F (200°C) for 20–25 minutes. Return them to the stove top. Turn up the heat. Shake your chili-infused vinegar and give the wings a good squirt. Stir with a wooden spoon, then remove the wings with tongs to a serving platter. Finish the sauce with a small amount of beer and 2–3 tbsp butter, and serve it with the wings. Drink the remaining beer with the wings.

PEOPLE GET HOOKED ON CHILIES BECAUSE THE BRAIN RESPONDS TO THE BURNING TASTE BY RELEASING ENDORPHINS THAT MAKE YOU FEEL HAPPY!

THE MOST

SPICES:

WHOLE IN

QUANTITIES

IN A COOL PLACE.

OUT OF THE LIGHT

KEEP THEM IN AIRTIGHT CONTAINERS
TO STAND GRIND THEM YOURSELF

SPICES

// Don't buy one of those huge discount containers with a lifetime supply of ground cinnamon. Spices lose their punch quickly—within six months. And when you're buying a spice blend, such as curry powder, try out a few to find out what you like. Their flavors can vary dramatically.

HOW TO TOAST AND GRIND YOUR OWN SPICES
///
> Preheat a nonstick omelet pan or small skillet over medium heat.
> Toast your spices for 1–2 minutes, tossing them in the pan just until it starts to lightly smoke and you can smell the fumes rising off the surface.
> Remove from the heat and transfer the spices out of the pan immediately or they will continue to burn.
> Grind them in a coffee grinder, or for small quantities grind with a mortar and pestle.
> If you don't have a grinder or mortar and pestle, sandwich the toasted spices between a piece of folded parchment paper, and return it to the cooled pan you used for toasting. Smash the spices up with your hand, and rub them around in a circle a little bit to release their essence.
///

RECIPE // SOUTHWESTERN SPICE RUB
> Mix together 3 tbsp ground annatto seed or paprika, ¼ cup each unrefined granulated sugar and salt, 2 tbsp ground cumin, 1 tbsp ground caraway, 2 tsp each turmeric and onion powder, 1 tsp each habanero chili powder and ground black pepper, and ¼ tsp celery seed. Store in an airtight container in a cool, dark place. Use for any broiled, grilled, or sautéed meat, chicken, or fish.

YOU ARE WHAT YOU FREEZE

// YOUR FREEZER IS THE BEST WAY TO MAKE SURE YOU ARE EATING HEALTHY AND CLEAN, EVEN WHEN YOUR NORMALLY BUSY LIFE SHIFTS INTO OVERDRIVE. KEEP THE FREEZER FULL AND WELL ORGANIZED—JUST LIKE YOUR LIST OF EMAIL CONTACTS—SO YOU WILL ALWAYS HAVE WHAT YOU NEED AT YOUR FINGERTIPS WHEN YOU WANT TO EAT SOMETHING GOOD, AND FAST.

THE COLD FACTS

//

> A full freezer is important. If it's not full, it's not running at maximum efficiency. You can save energy—and unnecessary car trips to the store—by keeping your freezer insulated with lots of good things to eat.
> Make your own convenience food. You will save money, and eat better.
> Label and date your frozen foods, and keep an eye on what's in there to make sure things don't get too old. The best way to do that is skip the cooking at least once a week and eat something from the freezer.
> If you're serious about your freezer, invest in a vacuum-pack sealer so you can freeze your food airtight and fresh, without bulking up your freezer with a bunch of clunky plastic containers. Remember that removing the air from bags and containers is vital to prevent oxidation of the food, which will cause it to turn brown.

//

MAX FREEZER STORAGE TIMES

///

> Fruit and veggies: 12 months
> Meat and poultry: 12 months
> Fish: 3 months
> Smoked fish: 2 months
> Bread: 6 months
> Cooked rice: 6 months
> Cooked legumes: 12 months
> Cooked pasta (undercooked or it will be too soft on thawing): 2 months
> Stock: 3 months
> Sauces: 3 months

///

FREEZING VEGGIES AND FRUIT

//

> Buy what's in season, and store it for darker days.
> Sealed bags of precut vegetables are a great thing to have in the freezer—
but only if you plan on cooking them. Don't freeze veggies you expect
to eat raw. And unless you blanch them first, only store for a week or two.
> Small bags of frozen chopped onions are a great time-saver.
> Green beans, broccoli, cauliflower, asparagus, peas, and sliced
mushrooms all freeze well.
> Making a stir-fry? Chop double the vegetables and freeze half for next time.
> Frozen berries are fabulous in a smoothie and don't need to be thawed first.

//

FREEZING COOKED GRAINS AND BEANS

//

> Nothing speeds up a stir-fry like having the rice already cooked and ready to go. Keep small sealed bags of cooked brown rice in the freezer for a healthy accompaniment to your stir-fries and sautés.

> For a satisfying, no-effort side dish, reheat 2 cups frozen cooked rice with an ice cube of chicken stock, a drizzle of olive oil or a pat of butter, and some herb salt (see page 93).

> Frozen cooked beans are good to add to a quick pot of chili or soup.

> A handful of cooked lentils or pearl barley can up the heartiness of practically any stew or soup. Add them in the final stages of cooking so they don't become overcooked.

//

LABEL EVERYTHING CLEARLY. THERE'S NOTHING WORSE THAN THAWING OUT A PACKAGE OF WHAT YOU THOUGHT WAS PASTA SAUCE TO FIND THAT IT'S APPLESAUCE.

FLAVOR CUBES

// These are a quick way to add depth and flavor to your recipes. Fill ice cube trays with juice—carrot, beet, or lemon, for example—or soup stock or another preparation. When they're frozen, transfer the cubes to an airtight bag. Then toss a cube or two straight into a dish as you cook. Opposite are some of my favorite cubes for flavoring soups, sauces, or casseroles. Freeze them for up to three months.

// Trader Joe's market sells awesome little trays of frozen chopped herbs and crushed garlic produced by Kibbutz Dorot in Israel. The tiny little cubes pop right out of the tray, and in cooked recipes you would never know the herbs and garlic had been frozen.

RECIPE // GARLICKY CHILI-CHICKEN CUBES

> Combine 4 cups good chicken stock, 2 tbsp puréed garlic, 1 tbsp dried chili flakes, 2 tbsp long grain rice, and ½ cup English peas (blanched fresh or thawed frozen). Bring to a boil, then simmer to cook the rice. Purée in a food processor or bar blender (it's okay if it's slightly lumpy). Let cool, then add some chopped fresh mint or basil. Pulse one more time to purée the herbs (it will be a sexy green color).

RECIPE // MOROCCAN CARROT-HARISSA CUBES

> Boil 8 cups carrot juice to reduce by half. Toast 2 tsp caraway seeds with 1 tsp cumin seeds until fragrant. Add 1 tbsp dried chili flakes and toast for another minute, then add 1 cup roasted eggplant purée, 1 tbsp each puréed garlic and fresh ginger root, and the reduced carrot juice. Bring to a boil and season. Purée in a bar blender. If you want a really smooth texture, pass through a strainer.

RECIPE // MELLOW MISO BROTH CUBES

> Bring 2 cups white miso broth, 2 cups white or yellow corn pulp (mashed kernels), 1 cup white vegetable stock, and 1 cup rice milk to a boil with 2 tbsp minced pickled ginger, 1 tbsp minced garlic, and 1 tsp cayenne. Reduce until thick enough to coat the back of a spoon. Purée (or not, if you enjoy texture). Add 1 cup minced, sautéed shiitake mushrooms and 3 tbsp minced fresh chives.

RECIPE // TOMATO-BASIL CUBES

> Slowly cook 2 super-fresh garlic cloves, sliced really thin, in 3 tbsp olive oil, without browning, until the garlic has melted into the oil. Add 2 tbsp red wine vinegar and let mingle, then add 1 tsp sugar. After a little bubble action, cool it down with crushed tomato pulp (4 or 5 good heirloom tomatoes, vine-ripes, or Romas passed through the grinder attachment of an electric stand mixer) and 2 cans good organic vegetable juice. Bring to a boil. Stir in the picked leaves from a bunch of basil. Purée or leave chunky.

FREEZING PASTA SAUCES, SOUPS, AND STOCK

//
> Only a fool would make a single serving of pasta sauce or soup. Always make a big full pot, and freeze the leftovers in useful-size containers.
> Soups hold up really well after freezing and reheating. They come back to life beautifully. To freeze soup, cool it gradually in the refrigerator and then transfer it to the freezer. Before freezing, make sure to wipe any condensation from the outside of the container.
> I like to freeze soup in smallish containers, for individual servings of instant gratification. You can even take these directly from the freezer to work with you, and reheat them at lunch time.
> After you make a roasted chicken, freeze up the leftover skin and bones in a bag to make a quick chicken stock kit for later. You can even freeze up the carrot sticks, sliced onion, and celery in advance, so when you want to make the stock, all you have left to do is season, add water, and boil!
//

THE 3 WAYS I FREEZE STOCK
//
> In ice cube trays for quick-hit flavor infusions to sauces and meat dishes.
> In 1-cup containers for use in recipes that call for stock.
> In 1-quart (1-liter) containers for use as a base for new soups.
//

RECIPE // COOL AND SPICY TOMATO SOUP

> Pulp 4 peeled and seeded nice-size tomatoes (pass through the grinder attachment of an electric stand mixer), followed by 1 cup peeled, seeded English cucumber and 1 serrano or jalapeño chili (seeded). Soften 1 minced shallot in 4 tbsp olive oil. Add the vegetable pulp along with 2 tbsp Banyuls vinegar and 1 tsp freshly ground cumin. Bring just to a boil. Purée in a bar blender until super-ultra-smooth (or leave it chunky). Pour into freezer container(s), cool, and freeze for up to 3 months.

To serve, thaw the soup and season. For each portion, purée ½ cup arugula leaves with 1 tbsp vegetable stock and ¼ tsp lemon juice until smooth—not too long or the heat from the motor will turn your arugula black. Serve the soup garnished with the puréed arugula in the center, a drizzle of extra virgin olive oil, and shaved Parmesan. Serves 4

RECIPE // CARAMELIZED MUSHROOM SAUCE

> Sauté 2lb (900g) crimini mushrooms, sliced medium-thick, in ¼ cup olive oil with a seasoning of pepper. Once they're golden brown, add 2 small shallots and 1 small white part of leek (all minced) and cook until translucent. Add 1 tsp smoked Spanish paprika, a small pinch of celery seed, 1 tsp ground cumin, ½ tsp ground fennel, and 1 tbsp grated orange zest, followed by ½ cup sherry vinegar. Stir well, then reduce until almost dry. Add 3 quarts (3 liters) good, strong, clear chicken or vegetable stock. Bring to a boil, then simmer to reduce by two-thirds. Strain. Pour into 2-cup freezer containers, cool, and freeze for up to 3 months.

Reheat to serve, then taste and season. Whisk in 1 tbsp chilled butter for the Frenchy effect or olive oil to go Mediterranean. This sauce goes really well with roasted pork, chicken, turkey, or lamb. Makes about 8 cups

THE 3 STEPS TO WRAPPING MEATS AND FISH FOR THE FREEZER

1 WRAP THE ITEM IN PLASTIC WRAP, THEN WHITE BUTCHER PAPER OR ALUMINUM FOIL

2 LABEL CLEARLY WHAT IS INSIDE AND DATE IT

3 SEAL THE PACKAGE IN AN AIRTIGHT BAG, SQUEEZING OUT ALL THE EXCESS SO NO AIR POCKETS REMAIN: AIR CONTAINS MOISTURE, WHICH TURNS TO FROST

FREEZING MEATS AND FISH

///

> When you take the time to go to a good butcher or fish market, it makes sense to buy in bulk so you can freeze individual-sized portions for later. This is where a vacuum sealer is particularly useful, but a high-quality locking freezer bag will work fine, too.

> Time-saver: When you make a tasty marinade, whip up an extra batch and toss it in a freezer bag with some fresh meat, fish, or poultry to freeze for another day. By the time the meat has thawed for cooking, it has been marinated, too.

> I'm known to hoard things when I find something great in season. This is especially true for wild salmon. In a good tight-sealed package, it will keep for six months in the freezer. But in my house, it's always gone before that.

> Artisanal sausages (made fresh without sodium nitrate and sodium nitrite, and other unnatural preservatives) are ideal to keep in the freezer. They thaw quickly, and a good sliced sausage or two can elevate soups, pastas, omelets, and frittatas to hearty, full-meal status. They're also great to throw on the grill or pan-fry for a quick delicious sandwich. For added convenience and good health, look for low-fat sausages that have been smoked or precooked, so you can safely add them to your soup or pasta with just a quick reheat.

> Always thaw meat, poultry, fish, and seafood in the refrigerator to make sure they stay fresh. This means you will need to remember to transfer them from the freezer to the refrigerator a day or two before you want to use them. Meats that are still partly frozen when cooked develop a rubbery consistency.

> Keep in mind that at the supermarket, a lot of the fish, poultry, and meats has been previously frozen and thawed—especially seafood. Make sure you know what you're buying, and if something has already been frozen, don't refreeze it (unless you cook it first).

///

OUR REFRIGERATORS, OURSELVES

// YOUR REFRIGERATOR IS WHAT'S GOING TO MAKE OR BREAK YOU AS FAR AS BEING ABLE TO EAT WELL. IN MY REFRIGERATOR, THERE ARE MORE CONDIMENTS THAN ANYTHING ELSE. THEY TAKE UP A WHOLE SHELF OF THEIR OWN. BUT WHEN IT COMES TO EATING CLEAN ON THE FLY, THERE'S NOTHING MORE IMPORTANT THAN A FRIDGE STOCKED WITH WHATEVER IS FRESH AND IN SEASON.

THE SALAD CRISPER

// When you have a salad in the crisper all washed and ready to go, you can literally grab a handful of clean greens right out of the refrigerator. Now there's absolutely no excuse for failing to include a salad with your meal. I also keep a steady supply of cabbage, broccoli, cucumber, and bell peppers in the crisper all the time, too.

THE BEST WAY TO MAKE SURE YOU EAT YOUR RAW GREENS
///
> Buy the greens prewashed, and wash them again when you get home
from the market. Wholehead greens are good too, but they will require
more advance work.
> Rinse your greens aggressively in cold water. Spin them dry in a salad
spinner, and store them in your crisper in a clean sealed container.
(I suggest you simply save a few of those plastic clamshell containers
from the store and reuse them again and again.)
> You don't want to keep your greens sitting around in the refrigerator for
more than a week; they become limp and unappetizing. So eat them up!
///

CARROTS FOR SNACKING
// Those prepeeled baby carrots are a fine convenience item, but they
get white and scaly if you don't take good care of them. To keep them fresh
and crisp, remove them from the original bag, rinse well, and store in a
sealed container with a few teaspoons of fresh water. This will help retain
their color and crispness. If you want a fuller-flavor carrot, buy medium-
sized carrots by the bunch at your local farmers' market, peel them, and
store them the same way for a quick crudité.

TOMATOES. DON'T REFRIGERATE
// An important exception to my refrigerator storage rule is tomatoes.
I always store them on the countertop instead of in the fridge. They
maintain their natural sweetness this way, and I think they actually
taste better at room temperature.

MILK. IT'S WHOLE FOR ME

// Health establishments will disagree, but I'm a whole milk guy. I like my milk to taste like milk, and I think whole-milk yogurt is hearty, beneficial, and satisfying. In my mind, whole foods of any kind—the way they occur in nature—are better for your body than scientifically engineered, processed, fat-reduced food byproducts. That goes for milk, too.

// Watching your fat intake? Pick your evil. I would much rather drink a glass of whole milk, or have a great yogurt parfait, than wolf down a couple of cheeseburgers. Of course, if you have particular medical reasons for maintaining a low-fat diet, please consider your own health above my personal preferences!

// Organic milk is best. Second-best is milk that comes from cows not treated with the hormone rBST, which boosts milk production. If a milk is rBST-free, it will be clearly labeled. Otherwise, you can be pretty sure the cow was on hormones when she made your milk.

NOT FROM THE COW

// If you have problems digesting dairy products and need a substitute, or if you're cooking for someone who does, I prefer rice milk over soy milk. Soy milk tastes chalky. Rice milk has a cleaner finish.

EGGS. ONLY THE BEST

// For health and humanitarian reasons, I only buy eggs from cage-free chickens. Eggs from cage-free chickens that were fed flax seed in their diet are even better, because that means the eggs have more healthful Omega-3 fatty acids.

IT'S WORTH CROSSING THE ROAD FOR HIGH-QUALITY EGGS.

YOGURT. I LOVE IT

//

> Always keep some plain, organic yogurt in the refrigerator. It's great for cooking, but even better for eating.

> I eat yogurt plain or I flavor it with fresh fruit, preserves, or fruit concentrates.

> The live cultures in fresh yogurt help your body to digest food efficiently, and serve to maintain the colonies of healthy bacteria that live in your intestinal track.

> Look for organic yogurt, from a local dairy if possible, made with whole milk. Check the label to make sure it has several live cultures.

> Yogurt is a good breakfast or snack food, and it makes a lovely dessert layered with beautiful fruits and nuts and drizzled with honey.

> Yogurt and seasonings make a great coat for baked fish or poultry (see my recipe on page 206), and a fresh, light base for sauces.

//

YOGURT IS AN IDEAL CHOICE FOR QUICK, HEALTHY EATING.

CHEESE, PLEASE!

// When it comes to cheese, I recommend small quantities of high quality. There are good mainstream cheeses available on the market, but there's a lot of junk out there, too. Don't waste your calories on bad cheese. Save up for the good stuff, and have a couple of bites with a glass of wine while you're making dinner or checking emails. Or serve a cheese plate to finish a special dinner for your friends.

// After my dinner guests go home, I don't throw out the little odds and ends left over on the cheese plate. I put them all into a sealed tub in the refrigerator. When I have enough little bites saved up, I cut off any blue fuzzy parts and make a batch of my mystery fondue. (Don't use extra firm cheeses for this, only the soft ones with a good melting quality.) I like to melt a pan of fondue for Kimmie and me to enjoy while I'm working on something in the kitchen. That way she'll stay and read the paper, and keep me company.

RECIPE // MYSTERY FONDUE

> Sauté some chopped shallots and garlic in a small saucepan. Toss in whatever herbs or spices suit your fancy (I like dried mustard seed). Add 1–2 cups white wine—depending on how much cheese you have—and simmer until it reduces by half. Throw in the cheese and stir until the fondue is smooth and creamy. Slice up a handful of bread cubes for dipping, and you've got yourself a snack.

FRESH FROM THE SEA

// There should regularly be fresh, wild-caught fish in your refrigerator, but never kept for more than a day or so. Fish should be purchased as close as possible to the day you intend to prepare it. If you can't cook it right away, or if you find a great deal on fresh fish in the market, freeze it in a tightly sealed bag for later.

// I never buy farm-raised fish because I think it causes a great deal of pollution, and can contain unseemly levels of pollutants. Rather, I prefer to buy what's available fresh and locally. When the discount warehouse store in my neighborhood is selling fresh, wild-caught Copper River salmon, I buy them out and seal it up in smaller quantities for the freezer.

// If I'm going to freeze a large piece of salmon that I know is destined for the wood-burning grill, I season it up in advance. (Every little step counts in a busy day!) Then all I have to think about before we actually eat it is what to serve along with it.

// Truly fresh seafood is hard to find. Most of the shrimp and scallops available on the market are previously frozen. It's okay to buy them frozen and keep in the freezer. Thaw seafood on the day you're going to use it, and rinse it thoroughly with cold running water in a colander.

EAT ONLY WHAT WE CAN TAKE FROM THE SEA IN GOOD CONSCIENCE.

BE A RESPONSIBLE FISH CONSUMER

// It's critically important to take responsibility for the consequences of what we take from the sea. As developing nations become wealthier, and as the health benefits of consuming fish become more widely understood, the world's appetite for fish is skyrocketing. We have to learn to wait our turn, and eat only what we can take from the sea in good conscience, or soon there will literally be nothing left.

// Be a nosy, scrupulous fish consumer. Ask hard questions, and be willing to walk away if you don't find something that meets your standards. I don't buy any seafood that doesn't meet the Monterey Bay Aquarium's sustainable fishing guidelines (see page 255), and you shouldn't either.

"UNCURED" DELI MEATS

// The preservatives sodium nitrate and sodium nitrite are big no-no's in my book, so those highly processed sandwich meats you grew up on are officially off-limits. But that doesn't mean you can't have a good turkey or salami sandwich when the urge strikes you.

// An increasing number of sustainable-farmed, "uncured" (or "naturally cured") deli meats are available now, many using celery juice as a natural, healthy preservative. You can find them at health food stores and some of the more health-conscious grocery chains, including Whole Foods. Their shelf-life is much shorter than processed lunch meats, but then again, they taste better so you won't mind eating them up quickly. They're not going to last for two months in your fridge, but you're not going to damage your health either. It's an easy trade-off, if you ask me.

// If you can't find "uncured" turkey, ham, roast beef, salami, hot dogs, bacon, or turkey bacon at your local stores, they are worth asking for. You just might be the one who tips the scales and encourages your merchants to make some new, healthy choices available for the whole community to try out and enjoy.

// Larry loved a good fast-food sandwich from Subway. So when I was cooking for Google I had to come up with lunch meats that tasted like they were processed, but weren't. In those days I had to be pretty aggressive to find vendors of "uncured" deli meats, but today they are much easier to find.

CONDIMENTS

// I have more condiments in my refrigerator than anything else. I think condiments should be no exception to smart eating. Be conscious of what ingredients are in there, and what your threshold is for buying garbage.

MY FAVORITE CONDIMENTS
///

> **Miso paste**. I use light-colored miso pastes in spring and summer months, and red and dark-colored misos in the winter and fall. They are great as a liquid base for vegetarian soups or sauces. Use about 1 tsp per cup of liquid.
> **Fermented dry black beans**.
> **Truffle oil and truffle butter**.
> **Indian chutneys**. I really like Major Gray's Indian-style mango chutney. I mix it with Dijon mustard as a spread for chicken sandwiches. It works well in chicken salad that way as well.
> **Japanese mayo**. My favorite, most versatile "secret sauce" is a sweet Japanese mayonnaise in a squeeze bottle called Kewpie. It was my best spread in the panini bar at Google. Spread on the outside of the bread instead of butter, it made for a deliciously crisp toasted sandwich.
> **Tartar sauce**.
> **Cocktail sauce**.
> **Mustard**. Lots of different mustards.
> **Ketchup**. I know some people who will make their own ketchup, but come on. Ketchup is out there. It's been proven. Spend your time on other things.
///

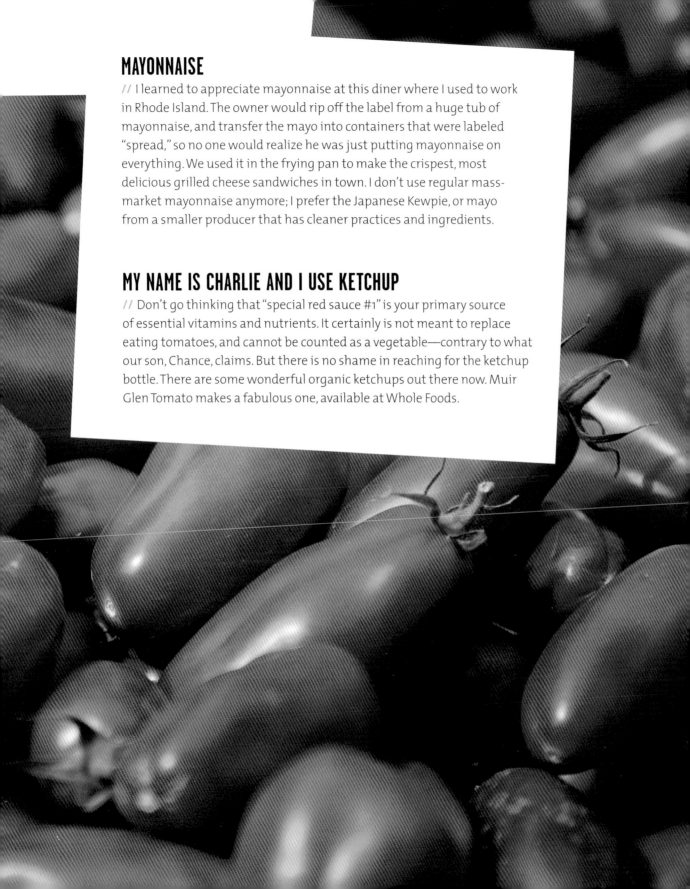

MAYONNAISE

// I learned to appreciate mayonnaise at this diner where I used to work in Rhode Island. The owner would rip off the label from a huge tub of mayonnaise, and transfer the mayo into containers that were labeled "spread," so no one would realize he was just putting mayonnaise on everything. We used it in the frying pan to make the crispest, most delicious grilled cheese sandwiches in town. I don't use regular mass-market mayonnaise anymore; I prefer the Japanese Kewpie, or mayo from a smaller producer that has cleaner practices and ingredients.

MY NAME IS CHARLIE AND I USE KETCHUP

// Don't go thinking that "special red sauce #1" is your primary source of essential vitamins and nutrients. It certainly is not meant to replace eating tomatoes, and cannot be counted as a vegetable—contrary to what our son, Chance, claims. But there is no shame in reaching for the ketchup bottle. There are some wonderful organic ketchups out there now. Muir Glen Tomato makes a fabulous one, available at Whole Foods.

HOMEMADE CONDIMENTS

RECIPE // CHUTNEY-YOGURT CRUST

> Mix mango chutney to taste with plain yogurt and a little turmeric. Coat some salmon in that, cover it, and let it sit in the refrigerator for a couple of hours. Then broil it. The chutney-yogurt mix browns up nicely—like a toasted marshmallow—and makes a really good crust.

RECIPE // CRUSTY MISO GLAZE

> Blend miso paste in the food processor with a little bit of sake, toasted sesame oil, and Dijon mustard, or ginger and garlic. Spoon it over fish, let it marinate for a day, and then broil it. If you want some heat, use red miso paste and put a little cayenne in there too. If you're using white miso, try adding a pinch of ground coriander or cumin. Serve the fish with minced green onion (scallion) and steamed brown rice.

RECIPE // JAPANESE MAYO COATING

> Stir sweet Japanese mayo with a little bit of miso paste and wasabi powder, and spread over fish or chicken before broiling.

RECIPE // KETCHUP GLAZE

> Flavor organic ketchup with a small amount of Chinese five-spice, dry sherry, and tamari, and you have a kick-ass glaze to put over salmon that is being broiled.

RECIPE // ROASTED JALAPEÑO KETCHUP

> Roast the hell out of some jalapeños, then skin and seed them. Put into a bar blender, add some orange juice, ground cumin, and ketchup, and purée. Transfer to a container and keep refrigerated.

CURRY PASTES AND FISH SAUCE

// I have fallen in love with the complicated flavor profiles you can find in ready-made curry pastes. Unlike the dry powders commonly used in India, Pakistan, and Sri Lanka, wet pastes are used in the cooking from Japan, Thailand, and Malaysia. In addition to the usual curry spices, pastes often include fish sauce, ginger root, galangal root, or citrus juices. They come in jars, tubes, or little buckets and have a long shelf life, but should be refrigerated after opening.

// Fish sauce is a great way to up the flavor profile of a lot of dishes. It can do wonders for a marinade or glaze for meat, poultry, or seafood, or can finish off a stir-fry. I started using fish sauce even in non-Asian dishes after realizing it was anchovies that made plain old Worcestershire sauce so flavorful. Now I shop around, tasting a lot of different fish sauces, because it helps deepen my dishes, giving them that full-mouth flavor known in Japanese philosophy as "umami," or the fifth taste. It's that feeling of well-being and satisfaction we find in things like chocolate, wine, and certain coffees. I think there's definitely a sense of well-being to be found in the right fish sauce. I particularly like the Three Crabs brand of fish sauce, which is a product from Thailand that is manufactured in Vietnam.

// Before using fish sauce, be conscious of who you're feeding. Vegetarians and people with seafood allergies should not be served fish sauce.

HOW TO ASK FOR FISH SAUCE

///
> In Vietnam, it's called "nuoc mam."
> In Thailand, they call it "nam pla."
> In the Philippines, ask for "patis."
///

STOCK UP ON STOCK

// I keep jars of homemade highly concentrated stock in my refrigerator. If you have time to spend the day properly reducing a hearty beef or chicken stock, you will reap the dividends for a long time to come. Called a "glace de vien," it's a concentrate that should be as dense as shoe polish. Use it a tablespoon at a time to bring full, yummy flavors to your soups, sauces, sautés, and grains. Stored in a clean, airtight jar in the fridge, it should be good for several months. It can also be frozen in ice cube trays.

RECIPE // GLACE DE VIEN

> Mince up 4 shallots and put in a pan with 1 tsp black peppercorns, 2 bay leaves, and 2 sprigs of thyme. Pour in ¼ bottle of good bourbon and boil until almost dry. Then add ½ bottle of port wine, and reduce that until it's almost dry. It will have a very sticky consistency. Add 4 cups of good, reduced, homemade beef stock and cook at a very low simmer for about 1 hour. Strain and continue to reduce in a small pot until syrupy. Pour into a small container for storage.

STORE UP SOME HERB SALT

// I like to make a big batch of this bright green herb salt at a time, then keep a small container on the countertop and refrigerate the rest in an airtight container for later.

// My herb salt is great to use at the end of cooking for sauces, and in mashed potatoes, stuffing, and soups. It gives an added punch to almost any really savory dish. I always add it right at the end so the fresh herb flavor is not cooked out. I steer away from using it in Asian-inspired dishes because it really muddles up those flavors.

RECIPE // HERB SALT

> Pick the leaves from a large sprig each of fresh thyme, oregano, and sage. Grind with 1 cup kosher salt and 2 peeled garlic cloves to make a paste. It will be bright green. Mix with 1 tsp each freshly grated nutmeg and white pepper. Work through large-hole chinoise strainer, if needed.

MORE KITCHEN ESSENTIALS

// FOR ME, THE FOODS YOU SHOULD HAVE ON HAND TO MAKE LIFE WORTH LIVING ARE GOOD BREAD, GOOD BEER, AND CHOCOLATE. GROWING SOME OF YOUR OWN FOOD IS ANOTHER ESSENTIAL TO AIM FOR—EVEN IF IT'S ONLY SOME HERBS ON A WINDOWSILL. AND OF COURSE GOOD KITCHEN TOOLS ARE WHAT MAKE COOKING A PLEASURE.

GOOD BREAD IS A MUST

// Like cheese, you should be willing to sacrifice quantity for quality in your diet. If you're going to eat bread, it should be handcrafted, whole grain, and delicious. Buy a good bread without preservatives, and freeze half or two-thirds of it for later. That way, it won't get stale and you can continue to enjoy it for a few more days.

RECYCLE YOUR BREAD

// Don't throw out the odds and ends of bread. A lot of good crusty bread in my house ends up in a bag in the freezer. When I have enough, I dice it up and make croûtons in the toaster oven. Sometimes the croûtons end up on a salad, sometimes they become stuffing. And sometimes they get thrown in the food processor and chopped into high-quality bread crumbs. The bread crumbs can be frozen again in small sealed bags.

BEER IS A HAPPINESS ITEM

// I'm not willing to give up beer. But I only buy local, handcrafted beer. If it's organic, even better. Most communities have their own locally-handcrafted beers. And even some decent local wines are available in unexpected parts of the country. I recently tasted a pleasant wine from Wisconsin. Make the effort to find what's brewing in your region. You might be happily surprised.

CHOCOLATE IS A NON-NEGOTIABLE PART OF MY LIFE

// Okay, so they don't grow cocoa beans in California, but our carbon footprints aside, you and I both know that we've gotta have chocolate. Where I live, we are lucky to have several outstanding local artisanal chocolatemakers to choose from. The beans come from far away, but the distribution is local.

IN SMALL AMOUNTS, THE CAFFEINE IN COCOA BEANS CAN STIMULATE YOUR MIND AND HELP YOU FOCUS.

4 BEST HERBS TO GROW AT HOME
1 CHIVES 2 BASIL

3 PARSLEY 4 MINT

GROW IT YOURSELF

// There is nothing more satisfying than cooking with food you have grown yourself. Whether it's a patch of lettuce in your garden or a little box of fresh parsley and chives growing in your window, your spirits and your dishes will be elevated if you can grow some of your food at home.

// Most common herbs are relatively easy to grow, and taste all the better when they are used fresh off the plant. Oregano tastes really good fresh, but it's not a quick grower. Check your local nursery to see what herbs will do well in your climate.

// The best veggies to grow yourself are salad leaves and tomatoes, if your local climate allows. Homegrown tomatoes are SO much better than store-bought that they are no doubt worth the effort.

// I don't have much room for gardening at home, so this year I'm growing my own cherry tomatoes in my kitchen with a hydroponic countertop grower. This really works and the tomatoes taste great.

MUST-HAVE EXTRA TOOLS

///

> Rice cooker
> Slow cooker
> Coffee grinders for spices (I have three coffee grinders: one for coffee, one for spices, and one for hot chilies)
> Food processor
> Hand or immersion blender

///

THE EASIEST MEAL EVER

// A slow cooker, or "crockpot," is one of the best time-savers in the kitchen. I use mine for cooking short ribs, stews, chili, and shanks, and for those large, hearty, inexpensive cuts of meat that take a long time to soften up. There's no need to go all Julia Child over those meats with a day's worth of braising and the big bunch of fuss. Just sear the meat in the morning, put it in the slow cooker, and throw in some herbs, onions, and celery. Add a little boiling stock or other liquid (about half the amount you would normally add) and let the meat cook on low heat all day. When you come home, the house will smell great and your dinner will be ready.

A MANDOLIN SLICER FOR GARLIC

// If you want to buy yourself a present, I think a Japanese mandolin slicer is a great extra tool to have. I hate peeling a clove of garlic and putting it on the cutting board to slice it, because it stinks up the board and the knife and my fingers. I can put my little mandolin slicer right over whatever I'm cooking, and cut the garlic right into the pan. If I were making a sauce, and didn't want the look of garlic slices, I would use a garlic press instead of the mandolin.

SAVE YOUR CONTAINERS, SAVE THE EARTH

// Recycling is a game in my house. We're always trying to ask ourselves: How can we reuse this? If we can't reuse it, we recycle it. When a food product comes swaddled in a lot of nonrecyclable packaging, your best choice is not to buy it.

// I am a big fan of recycled jars and plastic containers for my storage needs, particularly in the freezer. Just make sure they're dishwasher-clean before you reuse them. And always label the contents clearly with an indelible marker so you can tell what's in there without opening the container and exposing it to potential freezer burn.

// I think plastic is fine for storage purposes, but I don't ever reheat my food in plastic containers. The recycled tubs may not have been specifically engineered for high temperatures, and you never know when something might leak chemicals into your food when heated. Remove frozen food from the plastic container—run hot water along the outside of the container—and slide into a glass, metal, or earthenware dish. Or, thaw in the refrigerator until the food can be poured into a pot for reheating.

NO NUKES, PLEASE!

// I recommend not using a microwave oven. I believe in heating my food the old-fashioned way. I know you're busy, but be smart about your kitchen time. Pour yourself a glass of wine, and take that time while the food reheats to check your email, read the newspaper, plan tomorrow's dinner, or call a friend.

EVERYTHING IN MODERATION

// In the early days, Google did have a tendency to smell like a frat house. Those engineers never went home. There were piles of laundry strewn about, and mats all over the floor. I used to think they had a lot of pets there because of all those mats, but it turned out that's where they were sleeping. The engineers would play roller hockey out in the parking lot, and then come rolling into my café all sweaty and dirty with their trays out for a meal. Once Google was able to hire some women, the guys finally started showering. That's when the place started to run more smoothly, too.

// There was this one Googler named Lori Park. She was a mouthy girl from Harvard, and we were good friends. Lori was the one who got them to start printing up some women's t-shirts at Google. They had t-shirts for everything there. She's also the one who got me to cut back on the big meat and potato menus. At Lori's urging, I started offering a more diverse menu with a lot of salads, and I opened a panini bar. Both were really popular, but it backfired in a way. People weren't eating salads instead of the big hearty meals I had cooked. A lot of them were eating the big hearty meals I cooked and having a sandwich or a salad on top of it.

// Well, wouldn't you know it, some people got fat. (Vast quantities of delicious, expensive food, lovingly prepared by an innovative chef, available free of charge, will have a tendency to do that to you!) So they hired a bunch of boot camp instructors to make them run around the parking lot in order to squeeze back into their cubicles. I wasn't supposed to know this, but the fat camp instructors were wearing t-shirts emblazoned with a red slash through a picture of my face. I thought it was funny, but I told them the same thing I'll tell you: It's not my fault.

// Food is good. Good, healthy food is even better. But we all know that too much food can kill you. Meanwhile, everything tastes better with a lot of fresh air and exercise. So walk to the market. Take the stairs. Run around the parking lot if you have to. And put back that panini if you already had lunch!

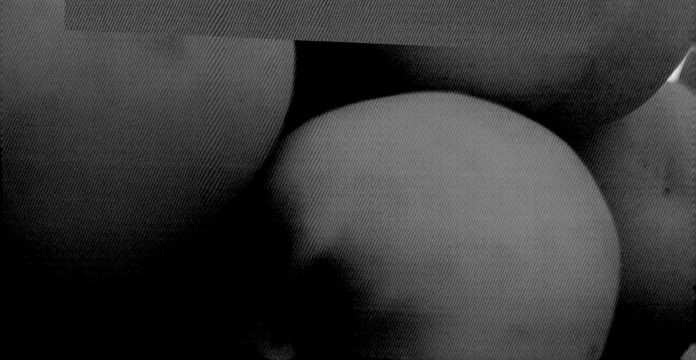

START MY DAY

SET THE COURSE OF YOUR DAY BY STARTING IT RIGHT. IF YOU KNOW YOU'LL BE BUSY AND WANT TO POWER UP, OPT FOR WHOLE GRAINS, YOGURT, FRESH FRUIT, AND GREEN TEA OVER SAUSAGE, EGGS, AND COFFEE. CONSIDER BREAKFAST AN INVESTMENT IN YOUR DAY. IF YOU ONLY HAVE COFFEE, YOU'RE NOT HELPING ANYONE EXCEPT THE GUY WHO SOLD YOU THE COFFEE.

BLACK AND BLUE YOGURT FRU FRU >>

SERVES 1 /// PREP TIME: 6 MINUTES /// COOK TIME: 0

1 tbsp toasted sliced almonds
2 tsp orange-blossom mountain honey
¼ cup blueberries
½ cup Greek-style yogurt
¼ cup blackberries
¼ tsp ground cinnamon

> Put the toasted almonds at the bottom of a sundae glass and drizzle
1 tsp of the honey over them. Put the blueberries on top and then half the
yogurt. Spoon in the blackberries and then the remaining yogurt. Drizzle
with the rest of the honey and dust with cinnamon. Chill overnight, and
enjoy first thing in the morning.

// This dish looks best served in a sundae glass and made the night before
you want to eat it.

DREAMY PEACH SMOOTHIE

SERVES 1 /// PREP TIME: 5 MINUTES /// COOK TIME: 0

1 peach, pitted and diced
4 large strawberries, hulled
1 banana, cut in pieces
⅛ tsp ground cinnamon
1 cup thick vanilla yogurt
1 cup crushed ice
Small fresh mint sprig for garnish

> Put all the ingredients into a blender. Blend until thick and smooth.
Pour into a glass, garnish with a small mint sprig, and serve.

CITRUS CRUSHER

SERVES 4 /// PREP TIME: 5 MINUTES /// COOK TIME: 0
2 cups fresh ruby red or pink grapefruit juice
1 cup pineapple juice
1 cup fresh orange juice
Lime-flavored sparkling mineral water, chilled

> Prepare this the night before you want to drink it. Fill 12 sections of an ice cube tray with some of the grapefruit juice and freeze.

> Mix the pineapple, orange, and remaining grapefruit juices together and chill for several hours or overnight.

> When ready to serve, put three frozen cubes of grapefruit juice in each of four large glasses. Pour on the mixed juices, fill the glasses with sparkling lime-flavored water, and stir. Drink through a straw.

// With all smoothie recipes, it is best to use fresh-squeezed juices whenever possible. This smoothie can be spiked with vodka or gin, to make a great brunch party drink.

HAWAIIAN KITCHEN-SINK SMOOTHIE

SERVES 4 /// PREP TIME: 10 MINUTES /// COOK TIME: 0

4 bananas, cut in pieces
½ cup fresh orange juice
¼ cup apple cider
8oz (225g) can pineapple in natural juice
½ cup fresh or frozen blueberries
10–12 fresh or frozen strawberries
1 cup pineapple juice
14oz (400g) can coconut milk, chilled
1 cup plain yogurt
2 tbsp fresh lemon juice
4 tsp orange-blossom honey (optional)
12 ice cubes
4 small, fresh strawberries for garnish (optional)

> Put all the ingredients, except the ice cubes, in a blender, adding the honey if you want a slightly sweeter smoothie. Blend until smooth, dropping in the ice cubes a few at a time.

> Pour into glasses. If garnishing, make a small slit in each strawberry and push one onto the rim of each glass. Serve immediately.

// I make this for four people so I use the whole can of coconut milk and the can of pineapple. But you can make less, and keep the rest of the coconut milk and fruit in the fridge for another smoothie (use them up within a day or two).

JADE SMOOTHIE

SERVES 1 /// PREP TIME: 5 MINUTES /// COOK TIME: 0

¼–½ English cucumber
6 large, fresh mint leaves
½ cup apple cider
¼ cup lemon sorbet
4 ice cubes

> Cut a slice off the cucumber and reserve for garnish. Peel the cucumber and split it lengthwise, then scoop out the seeds with a teaspoon. Roughly chop the cucumber.

> Place in a blender with the remaining ingredients. Blend until smooth. Pour into a glass, garnish with the halved cucumber slice, and serve.

IF YOU DON'T HAVE TIME TO EAT YOUR BREAKFAST THEN DRINK IT.

SCREWY RABBIT ... THINK BRUNCH!

SERVES 2 /// PREP TIME: 5 MINUTES /// COOK TIME: 0

½ cup good vodka
½ cup fresh orange juice
½ cup fresh carrot juice
1 tbsp fresh lemon juice
2 washed baby carrots with the green tops intact (optional)

> Stir the vodka with the juices. Pour over ice in chilled highball glasses. Garnish each with a baby carrot, if desired, and serve.

// This is great for brunch or as an evening pick-me-up. I buy fresh carrot juice at the taquerias near my house so I don't have to go to the trouble and mess of making the juice myself.

THIS IS NOT ONE TO DRINK ON YOUR OWN OR FIRST THING IN THE MORNING.

SMOOTHIE SANDIA

SERVES 1 /// PREP TIME: 10 MINUTES /// COOK TIME: 0

Bar salt
3/4 cup fresh or frozen blueberries, plus a few for garnish
1/2 cup pineapple juice
1 tsp wild-blossom honey
1 large wedge of watermelon, peeled, seeded, and cubed

> Dip the rim of a glass in water and then in bar salt. Thread a few blueberries on a toothpick or cocktail skewer for garnish. Place the rest of the berries, the juice, honey, and watermelon in a blender, and mix on low speed until blended. Continue mixing, gradually increasing the speed, until smooth. Pour the smoothie into the glass and rest the skewer of berries on the rim.

// There's nothing more refreshing than a watermelon smoothie when the temperature outside is rising faster than Google on a good day at the market. Add a shot of tequila to turn this into a relaxing evening cocktail.

PEACEFUL BERRY MORNING SMOOTHIE

SERVES 1 /// PREP TIME: 4 MINUTES /// COOK TIME: 0

1 banana, cut in pieces
1/2 cup fresh or frozen strawberries
1/2 cup fresh or frozen raspberries
1/2 cup thick strawberry yogurt
1/2 cup cranberry juice cocktail or apple cider—
    or you can even go for orange juice if you prefer

> Place all the ingredients in a blender. Blend until smooth. Serve.

WAKE-UP SHAKE-ME-UP POWER SHAKE ≫

SERVES 1 /// PREP TIME: 8 MINUTES PLUS CHILLING /// COOK TIME: 0

½ cup strong-brewed black tea, chilled
½ cup rice milk
¼ cup fresh orange juice
1 small banana, cut in pieces
¼ cantaloupe melon, peeled, seeded, and diced
2 tsp wild-blossom honey
¼ cup fresh or frozen strawberries
An extra small sliver of melon for garnish

> Put all the ingredients in a blender. Blend until smooth. Pour into a large glass, garnish with a small sliver of melon on the rim, and serve.

// I often find smoothies to be a lot more invigorating and uplifting than a cup of coffee in the morning.

ORANGE CARROT CABARET

SERVES 1 /// PREP TIME: 10 MINUTES /// COOK TIME: 0

3 small ice cubes
2 apricots, pitted and sliced
½ papaya, peeled, pitted, and diced (or use frozen)
½ mango, peeled, pitted, and diced (or use frozen)
½ cup fresh carrot juice
1 tsp wild-blossom honey (optional)

> Put all the ingredients, except the honey, in a blender and blend until smooth. Taste and add the honey, if necessary, then blend for a few more seconds. Serve immediately in a frosted glass.

WASHINGTON NUTTY-BLUE SMOOTHIE

SERVES 1 /// PREP TIME: 5 MINUTES /// COOK TIME: 0

1 peach, pitted and sliced
1/4 cup fresh or frozen blueberries
1 cup vanilla yogurt, chilled
1/2 cup milk
1/2 tbsp smooth peanut butter
A pinch of kosher salt
1/4 tsp natural vanilla extract
A few chopped raw peanuts for garnish (optional)

> Put all the ingredients into a blender and blend until smooth. Pour into a tall glass, garnish with a few chopped peanuts, if desired, and serve.

ALL-AROUND NUTRITIONAL SUPERSTARS, BLUEBERRIES CAN IMPROVE CONCENTRATION, SO STOCK UP.

WAKE-UP BREAKFAST SMOOTHIE

SERVES 1 /// PREP TIME: 15 MINUTES /// COOK TIME: 0

½ cup plain yogurt
½ cup fresh carrot juice
⅓ cup fresh orange juice
1 ripe banana, cut in pieces
¼ cup chopped melon
1 tsp pickled ginger
1 tbsp royal jelly (optional)
2 or 3 ice cubes

> Put all the ingredients in a blender and blend until smooth. Pour into a tall glass and drink immediately.

MOUNT SHASTA FRUIT SMOOTHIE

SERVES 1 /// PREP TIME: 5 MINUTES /// COOK TIME: 0

1 nectarine or peach, pitted and sliced
1 banana, cut in pieces
2 tbsp wheat germ
4 tbsp fresh orange juice
½ cup thick vanilla yogurt
2 or 3 ice cubes

> Reserve a slice of nectarine or peach and a pinch of wheat germ for garnish, if desired. Put the remainder in a blender or food processor with the rest of the ingredients. Blend until smooth.

> Pour into a tall glass, garnish with the reserved slice of fruit and pinch of wheat germ, and serve.

 SMOOTHOCCINO

SERVES 1 /// PREP TIME: 5 MINUTES PLUS CHILLING /// COOK TIME: 0

1 cup brewed double-strength coffee, chilled
1/4 cup half-and-half, chilled
4 ice cubes
1/2 cup milk, chilled
Whipped cream (if you have company, or if you just want to treat yourself)
Ground cinnamon for garnish

> Put the coffee, half-and-half, ice cubes, and milk in a blender and blend until smooth and frothy. Pour into a glass coffee mug and add whipped cream, if feeling decadent. Dust with cinnamon before serving.

ZEN STRAWBERRY-ORANGE SMOOTHIE

SERVES 1 /// PREP TIME: 5 MINUTES PLUS CHILLING /// COOK TIME: 0

1/2 cup strong-brewed green tea, chilled
1/2 cup sliced strawberries
1/2 cup fresh orange juice
1/2 cup crushed ice
1/4 cup rice milk
1 tsp wild-blossom honey

> Put the tea in a blender. Reserve a few slices of strawberry for garnishing, if desired, and add the rest to the blender along with the remaining ingredients. Blend until smooth. Pour into a large glass. Garnish with the reserved sliced strawberries and serve.

FLUFFY SOY PANCAKES

MAKES 8 /// PREP TIME: 10 MINUTES PLUS STANDING ///
COOK TIME: ABOUT 25 MINUTES

1 cup unbleached all-purpose flour
1/2 cup soy flour
2 tsp baking powder
1/4 tsp kosher salt
1 tbsp unrefined granulated sugar
2 eggs, separated
1 1/4 cups milk
3 tbsp butter, melted
Canola oil

> Sift the flours with the baking powder and salt into a bowl. Beat
the sugar and egg yolks together in another bowl until thick and pale.
Gradually whisk in the milk and melted butter, and then the flour
mixture, whisking well until smooth. Cover and let stand for 30 minutes.

> Beat the egg whites until stiff. Gently fold into the batter using a metal
spoon, to retain the fluffiness of the egg whites.

> Heat a little oil in a skillet. Pour off the excess, then add about 2 tbsp
of the batter and spread out to make a 5in (12.5cm) pancake. Cook over
medium heat until golden underneath and bubbles appear and burst
on the surface. Flip over and cook the other side. Remove and keep warm
in a low oven while you cook the remaining pancakes.

> Serve hot, with fruit-infused pancake syrup and powdered sugar.

// Soy flour is another way of getting protein into your diet. You can
eat these pancakes and skip the bacon.

APRICOT MULTIGRAIN BREAKFAST

MAKES ABOUT 8 CUPS /// PREP TIME: 5 MINUTES /// COOK TIME: 0

2 cups rolled oats
2 cups millet or barley flakes
1/2 cup wheat germ
1/2 cup sesame seeds
1/2 cup raw peanuts, roughly chopped
1 cup raisins
1 cup dried apricots, chopped
2/3 cup dried banana slices, chopped if large
1/4 tsp ground cinnamon
2 tsp finely chopped crystallized ginger
1 tbsp unrefined light brown sugar

> Mix all the ingredients together and store in an airtight container. Serve with milk and/or plain Greek-style yogurt and a trickle of honey, if desired.

// For a hot breakfast, mix 1/2 cup of the cereal with 1/2 cup milk in a saucepan. Bring to a boil, then reduce the heat and simmer gently, stirring occasionally, until thick and creamy, about 3 minutes. Serve as above.

GRANOLA

MAKES ABOUT 8 CUPS /// PREP TIME: 5 MINUTES /// COOK TIME: 20 MINUTES

4 cups rolled oats
1/2 cup raw cashews
1/2 cup sunflower seeds
1/2 cup wheat germ
1/4 cup sesame seeds
1/4 cup toasted hemp seeds
1/2 tsp kosher salt
3/4 cup dried, unsweetened, flaked coconut (large)
1/4 cup canola oil
1/4 cup apple cider
4 tbsp orange-blossom honey
1/2 tsp natural vanilla extract

> Preheat the oven to 350°F (180°C). Mix all the dry ingredients together in a large mixing bowl. Mix all the wet ingredients together in a separate bowl, stirring until the honey has dissolved. Add to the dry ingredients and mix thoroughly.

> Spread evenly in two shallow baking pans. Bake until evenly golden brown, about 20 minutes, folding the browning granola from the edges into the center of the pans with a metal spatula after every 5 minutes.

> Remove from the oven and tip into an airtight container. Leave until the granola is cold, then put on the lid to seal. Store in a cool, dry place. Serve with fresh fruit and plain yogurt.

THE ENGINEERS AT GOOGLE CALLED THIS "CHARLIE'S MYSTICAL GRANOLA."

FRUITY SESAME-SEED GRANOLA

MAKES ABOUT 7 ½ CUPS /// PREP TIME: 5 MINUTES /// COOK TIME: 20 MINUTES

6 tbsp grapeseed oil
⅓ cup apple cider
¼ cup wild-blossom honey
1 ½ tsp ground cinnamon
1 cup rolled oats
1 cup sliced almonds
1 cup raw cashews
1 cup dried, unsweetened, shredded coconut
¾ cup sesame seeds
¾ cup raisins
¾ cup moist dried cranberries or blueberries

> Preheat the oven to 350°F (180°C). Put the oil, apple cider, honey, and cinnamon in a large saucepan and bring to a boil, stirring. Stir in the oats, nuts, coconut, and seeds until everything is coated well.

> Spread the mixture evenly in two baking pans. Bake until golden brown, about 20 minutes, folding the browning granola from the edges into the center of the pans with a metal spatula after every 5 minutes.

> Stir in the raisins and cranberries or blueberries. Leave until completely cold before storing in an airtight container.

// This is much better than any store-bought granola. I eat it as dessert or carry it instead of gorp (trail mix) when backpacking. It is very good eaten straight, with no milk. If you choose to make it with blueberries, I'm sure you will love the granola mixed with a small amount of milk and creamy peanut butter. This makes a wonderful high-in-protein snack for early morning or late night.

CREAMY BREAKFAST POLENTA

SERVES 4 /// PREP TIME: 5 MINUTES /// COOK TIME: 4–11 MINUTES

1 cup light cream
2 ½ cups milk
Pinch of kosher salt
1 cup coarse yellow cornmeal (polenta)
¼ cup unrefined light brown sugar, lightly packed
1 tbsp unsalted butter
½ tsp ground cinnamon
¼ cup currants or other dried berries
2 tbsp mascarpone or Neufchâtel cheese

> Combine the cream, milk, and salt in a heavy-based pan and bring almost to a boil. Add the cornmeal in a slow, steady stream, whisking constantly to keep the mixture smooth and free of lumps. Cook and whisk the mixture until it is thick, 3–10 minutes, adding more milk if the polenta becomes too thick. (Timing will vary depending on the cornmeal you use.) Stir in the brown sugar and butter with a wooden spoon and beat for 1 minute. Beat in the cinnamon and currants.

> Remove from the heat and beat in the mascarpone or Neufchâtel cheese. Serve immediately in individual bowls, with extra milk and some brown sugar, if desired.

// This takes a bit more time than oatmeal, but it's worth it, especially on cold, nasty mornings. It makes a delicious dessert, too.

POLENTA SETS A CALMING TONE FOR THE REST OF THE DAY.

BREAKFAST TACOS

SERVES 2 OR 4 /// PREP TIME: 15 MINUTES /// COOK TIME: 7 MINUTES

4 soft, yellow corn tortillas
1 tbsp butter
2 shallots, chopped
1 fresh, hot, red or green chili (such as a Thai chili), seeded and chopped
3oz (85g) cooked *carne asada* or leftover roast beef, shredded or chopped
6 dashes or so of your favorite hot sauce (see Google Hot Sauce, page 249)
½ cup cooked long grain rice
2 eggs, beaten
½ cup shredded green or napa cabbage or lettuce
½ cup grated *queso fresco* or mozzarella cheese (optional)

> Warm the tortillas according to the package directions.

> Meanwhile, melt the butter in a nonstick sauté pan and sauté the shallots until they are turning lightly golden, about 2 minutes. Add the chili and meat, and stir until the meat is beginning to crisp a little. Hit it with the hot sauce, then add the rice and toss a couple times until the rice is hot throughout. Turn down the heat, add the eggs, and cook, stirring, until scrambled but not too dry.

> Remove from the heat and divide among the tortillas. Top with the shredded cabbage and then the cheese, if using. Roll up and eat.

// I came up with these when I was really hungover one morning. When I was grabbing the eggs I saw a leftover piece of steak next to them and I said, I have a place for you! If you don't have any leftover beef, quickly sauté a small frying steak, cut in thin shreds.

QUICK APPLE-OATY THING

SERVES 1 /// PREP TIME: 10 MINUTES /// COOK TIME: 5 MINUTES PLUS STANDING

3/4 cup rolled oats
1 1/2 cups apple cider or water
1 small apple, cored and diced
2 tbsp of your favorite dried fruits, chopped if necessary
1 tbsp toasted pumpkin seeds
1 tbsp flaxseed oil
Wild-blossom honey
A large spoonful of thick plain or vanilla yogurt

> Combine the oats, apple cider or water, apple, dried fruits, and pumpkin seeds in a saucepan. Bring to a boil, then reduce the heat and simmer, stirring, until thick and the oats are cooked, about 5 minutes. The apple should still have some texture to it. Remove from the heat and let stand for 5 minutes.

> Stir in the flax oil and sweeten to taste with honey. Spoon into a serving bowl and top with the yogurt. Drizzle a little more honey over the top if you want a sweeter finish.

OATS ARE GREAT. THEY SLOW THE ABSORPTION OF GLUCOSE INTO THE BLOODSTREAM, GIVING YOU A STEADY RELEASE OF ENERGY.

CRANBERRY-ORANGE BREAD

MAKES 1 LOAF /// PREP TIME: 15 MINUTES /// COOK TIME: 1 ¼ HOURS

2 cups fresh or thawed frozen cranberries
½ cup unrefined granulated sugar
2 cups unbleached all-purpose flour
½ cup whole wheat flour
½ cup unrefined light brown sugar, lightly packed
2 tsp baking powder
½ tsp baking soda
½ tsp fine sea salt
Finely grated zest of 1 orange
Juice of 3 oranges
⅓ cup vegetable oil
1 egg
1 tsp natural vanilla extract
A little milk

> Preheat the oven to 350°F (180°C). Lightly oil a standard 9 by 5in (23 by 12cm) metal loaf pan. Dust the pan with flour and tap out the excess.

> Mix the cranberries and granulated sugar together in a small bowl. Set aside. In a separate bowl, mix the flours, brown sugar, baking powder, baking soda, and salt. Set aside.

> Whisk together the orange zest, juice, oil, egg, and vanilla extract. Add to the flour mixture and stir just until the ingredients are barely combined. Fold in the sugared cranberries. Add a little milk, if needed, to make a soft consistency that will drop from the spoon when it is gently shaken. Transfer the batter to the prepared pan and level the surface.

> Bake until well risen, golden, and firm to the touch, about 1 ¼ hours. A toothpick inserted in the center should come out clean. Let cool until just warm, then run a knife around the inside of the pan and unmold the loaf onto a wire rack to cool completely. Serve sliced and buttered.

BEETS WITH BACON AND CRUMBLED BLUE CHEESE

SERVES 2 /// PREP TIME: 10 MINUTES /// COOK TIME: ABOUT 10 MINUTES

4 slices of "uncured" applewood-smoked bacon
1 tbsp olive oil
1 red onion, halved and sliced
1 tbsp ground cumin
1 tbsp ground coriander
1 tsp smoked sweet paprika
4 tbsp Banyuls or sherry vinegar
3 large, fresh cooked beets, peeled and cut in wedges
1 tsp unrefined granulated sugar
Kosher salt and freshly ground black pepper
1/2 cup crumbled blue cheese
1 tbsp chopped fresh flat-leaf (Italian) parsley leaves

> Cook the bacon in a nonstick sauté pan until crisp. Remove from the pan, drain on paper towels, and roughly break up. Set aside.

> Remove all but 1 tbsp of the bacon fat from the pan, then add the olive oil and heat. Add the onion and sauté, stirring, until lightly golden, 2–3 minutes. Add the spices and vinegar, and then the beets. Toss gently until they are hot, about 5 minutes. Add the sugar and season to taste.

> Spoon the beets onto two plates. Sprinkle the bacon on top followed by the crumbled blue cheese and then the chopped parsley. Serve with whole grain bread.

HO CHI MINH CHICKEN AND SHRIMP

SERVES 1 /// PREP TIME: 10 MINUTES /// COOK TIME: 5 ½ MINUTES

1 tbsp vegetable or sunflower oil
1 cup Vietnamese vegetable mix (finely diced onion, green beans, and carrots)
½ tsp finely chopped lemongrass
1 small skinless, boneless chicken breast half, cut in thin strips
1 cup raw, peeled, small shrimp, deveined if necessary
½ tsp minced garlic
3 tbsp dark soy sauce
2 tsp rice vinegar
1 tsp palm sugar or unrefined light brown sugar
½ tsp toasted sesame oil
Freshly ground black pepper
¼ head romaine, shredded

> Heat the oil in a wok and stir-fry the mixed vegetables, lemongrass, and chicken for 2 minutes. Toss in the shrimp and stir-fry until they are pink, about 1 minute longer.

> Add the remaining ingredients, except the shredded lettuce, and stir-fry for 30 seconds.

> Pile the lettuce on a plate and spoon the chicken and shrimp mixture on top. Serve immediately.

// To turn this into a more substantial dinner dish, add 1 cup cooked rice noodles with the soy sauce and other flavorings.

CHILI-CILANTRO RICE

SERVES 4 /// PREP TIME: 20 MINUTES /// COOK TIME: 20 MINUTES

1 fresh habanero chili, seeded and roughly chopped
1 fresh jalapeño chili, seeded and roughly chopped
A large handful of fresh cilantro leaves, roughly chopped,
  plus a few torn leaves for garnish
1 tsp ground cumin
Juice of 1 lemon
½ tsp kosher salt
Freshly ground black pepper
2 tbsp olive oil
2 cups long grain rice
1 large white onion, chopped
2 celery ribs, chopped
2 carrots, chopped
5 cups vegetable stock
1 cup raw cashew nuts (optional)
1 tbsp butter

> Purée the chilies and chopped cilantro with the cumin, lemon juice, salt, and lots of pepper in a blender, stopping occasionally to scrape down the sides as necessary.

> Heat the oil in a heavy-based pan. Add the rice and sauté, stirring, until lightly golden, about 2 minutes. Add the onion, celery, and carrots, and sauté for 1 more minute, stirring. Stir in the spice paste and then the stock. Add the cashews, if using. Bring to a boil, stirring. Reduce the heat, partially cover, and simmer gently until the rice has absorbed the liquid and is just tender, about 20 minutes.

> Stir in the butter. Taste and add more seasoning, if necessary. Serve hot or cold, garnished with torn cilantro.

// When time is short, rather than making the paste, just add the minced chilies and half the cilantro with the other flavorings after sautéing the vegetables. Stir in the rest of the cilantro at the end of cooking.

DRAGON BREATH NOODLES

SERVES 4 /// PREP TIME: 10 MINUTES /// COOK TIME: ABOUT 5 MINUTES

1 tbsp vegetable oil
4 green onions (scallions), finely chopped
1 tsp dried chili flakes
2 tsp red miso paste
3/4 cup boiling water
2 garlic cloves, crushed
1 tbsp orange-blossom honey
1/2 tsp toasted sesame seeds
4 tbsp smooth peanut butter
3 tbsp tamari
1 tsp finely chopped pickled ginger
Juice of 1/2 lime
1lb (450g) fresh egg noodles
Sliced red chili or chopped red bell pepper for garnish

> Heat the oil in a pan. Add the green onions and sauté for 2 minutes. Add the remaining ingredients except the noodles. Cook, stirring, until thickened and smooth.

> Add the noodles and toss gently until they are hot, 2–3 minutes. Garnish with chili or bell pepper and serve, with a crisp green salad.

// These noodles are great on their own, and also work well with a piece of broiled or grilled fish.

ASPARAGUS AND MUSHROOM PIZZA

MAKES 4 PIZZAS /// PREP TIME: 25 MINUTES PLUS RISING /// COOK TIME: 20 MINUTES

3 cups unbleached bread flour

3 tbsp whole wheat flour

1/4 cup fine yellow cornmeal (polenta)

2 tsp kosher salt

Pinch of unrefined granulated sugar

1 package quick-rising active dry yeast

1 tbsp olive oil

1 1/2 cups warm water

FOR THE TOPPING

4oz (115g) thin asparagus spears, trimmed and halved lengthwise

Olive oil

4 cups sliced assorted mushrooms (have fun—use shiitakes, maitakes, chanterelles, portabellos, and even cultivated white mushrooms)

2 large shallots or 1 red onion, sliced

1 cup shredded Savoy cabbage

1 cup shredded Manchego cheese

1 cup shredded Asiago or other melting cheese (such as Swiss)

2 tbsp chopped fresh tarragon or basil leaves

2 tbsp snipped fresh chives

2 tbsp chopped fresh flat-leaf (Italian) parsley leaves

Kosher salt and freshly ground black pepper

> First make the dough. Mix the flours with the cornmeal, salt, and sugar. Stir in the yeast. Add the oil and then the water and mix to form a soft but not sticky dough. Knead gently on a lightly floured surface for 5 minutes. Place in an oiled plastic bag and let rise in a warm place until doubled in bulk, about 1 hour.

> Alternatively, put all the ingredients in a food processor or electric mixer fitted with the dough hook and run the machine until a ball of dough forms. Run it for 1 minute longer, to knead the dough. Wrap and let rise.

> Punch down the dough and knead briefly until smooth. Divide into four balls. Put each ball on an oiled baking sheet and press out with your fingers to stretch evenly to a round about 8in (20cm) in diameter. Cover with oiled plastic wrap and let rise for 30 minutes.

> Meanwhile, prepare the topping. Heat a ridged cast-iron grill pan. Brush the asparagus with olive oil and pan-grill, turning once, until bright green, slashed with brown, and just tender, about 4 minutes. Cut in short lengths on the bias and set aside.

> Heat 2 tbsp oil in the pan and sauté the mushrooms until softened, 1–2 minutes. Remove from the pan. Add another 1 tbsp oil to the pan and sauté the shallots and cabbage, stirring, until they are softening slightly, about 2 minutes.

> Preheat the oven to 425°F (220°C). Top the risen pizza bases with the cheeses, then the mushrooms, then the asparagus, and then the cabbage and shallot. Sprinkle with half the herbs. Drizzle with olive oil and season with a sprinkling of salt and a grinding of pepper. Bake until the crust is golden around the edges and crisp underneath, about 20 minutes. If necessary, swap the sheets halfway through cooking. Sprinkle with the remaining herbs before serving.

// For wood-grilled pizzas, shape your dough into four pieces and let rise, then place on the hot (not too hot) side of the open kettle grill. Cook for about 2 minutes. Brush with olive oil and season before turning over to the other side. Add the toppings. Lower the heat (close the vents or move the pizzas to a cooler part of the grill), close the lid, and cook until the topping is hot throughout and the cheeses have melted, about 5 minutes.

KHMER SPRING ROLLS

MAKES 12 /// PREP TIME: 1 HOUR /// COOK TIME: 0

6oz (175g) firm tofu, drained, lightly fried in a splash
   of canola oil, and cut in thin strips
1 carrot, grated
3 large napa cabbage leaves, finely shredded
4 green onions (scallions), finely chopped
12 fresh mint leaves, finely shredded
6 fresh Thai basil leaves, finely shredded
A handful of fresh cilantro leaves, chopped
2 garlic cloves, crushed
2oz (60g) pickled ginger, chopped
1 tbsp tamari
1 tbsp palm sugar or unrefined light brown sugar
2 tbsp mixed black and white sesame seeds
A few drops of hot sauce (Sriracha or Tabasco)
Freshly ground black pepper
12 spring roll wrappers
2oz (60g) daikon sprouts

> Place everything, except the spring roll wrappers and daikon sprouts,
in a bowl. Mix well and set aside to get happy.

> Put the spring roll wrappers in a shallow dish and cover with warm
water. Let soak for 30 seconds, then drain and dry on paper towels. Divide
the vegetable-tofu mixture among the wrappers, leaving a ½ in (1cm)
border all around except at the top.

> Fold up the bottom of one of the skins and start rolling up from one side.
When you get three-fourths of the way, place a small amount of daikon
sprouts on top of filling, then continue rolling up completely. Roll up the
rest of the spring rolls. Arrange on a serving platter.

// For a change from daikon sprouts, use bean sprouts and lay a few chive
stems on top when rolling.

CELERY ROOT AND MUSHROOM SOUP

SERVES 6 /// PREP TIME: 20 MINUTES /// COOK TIME: ABOUT 30 MINUTES

1 head celery root (celeriac), about 1 ½lb (675g)
Juice of ½ lemon
2 tbsp unsalted butter
1 small leek, white part only, finely chopped
1 shallot, finely chopped
8oz (225g) button mushrooms, thinly sliced
Leaves from 5 fresh thyme sprigs, finely chopped
4 tsp white wine vinegar
8 cups chicken stock
Kosher salt and freshly ground pepper
⅓ cup heavy cream
Freshly grated nutmeg

> Peel the celery root and cut into 1in (2.5cm) dice. Toss with the lemon juice and 2 tbsp water to prevent it from browning. Set aside.

> Heat the butter in a large pan. Add the leek and shallot. Sauté over low heat, stirring, until the vegetables are soft but not brown, about 3 minutes. Add the mushrooms and continue to cook gently, stirring occasionally, until they release their juices.

> Drain the celery root and add with half the thyme. Continue to cook gently, stirring, until the pan is almost dry, taking care not to brown anything. Add the vinegar and stir until the pan is almost dry again. Add the chicken stock and some salt and pepper and bring to a boil. Reduce the heat to medium and simmer until the liquid has reduced by about half and the vegetables are really tender, about 20 minutes.

> Purée the soup in a blender until smooth, then pass through a fine-mesh strainer back into a clean pan. Stir in the cream and season to taste with nutmeg, salt, and pepper. Reheat but do not boil. Ladle into bowls and sprinkle with the remaining thyme. Serve hot.

TURKEY-AVOCADO-CARROT WRAP

MAKES 1 /// PREP TIME: 10 MINUTES /// COOK TIME: 0

1 soft flour tortilla (preferably whole wheat, but plain will do)
½ avocado, halved and pitted
A squeeze of lemon juice
1 slice Monterey Pepper Jack cheese
2oz (60g) sliced, cooked turkey breast
A small handful of baby spinach leaves
1 small carrot, shredded
A little hot sauce (see Google Hot Sauce, page 249), optional

> Lay a sheet of wax paper on a board and place the tortilla on top. Scoop out the avocado flesh and crush with the lemon juice, then spread across the tortilla. Top with the cheese, then the turkey, then the spinach, and last the carrot. Approach wrapping the tortilla as if it were a clock: Begin to wrap from six o'clock, continuing to wrap until the tortilla has come full circle and now resembles a cone shape.

> Peel back, reach for your favorite hot sauce—if you feel like it—and enjoy.

// If you are preparing ahead, make these in the morning—don't try to put them together the night before or the spinach will wilt and the carrot will make the tortilla damp! You can add a handful of bean sprouts to the wrap, to feel really good about your lunch, but you'll have to roll it quite tightly to hold all that filling!

ONE OR TWO OF THESE IS A GREAT LUNCH ON THE RUN.

HEIRLOOM TOMATO AND BABY LEAF SALAD

SERVES 4 /// PREP TIME: 30 MINUTES /// COOK TIME: 30 MINUTES

2 slices of rye bread, cubed
2 tbsp milk
¼ cup quinoa, rinsed
½ cup corn kernels (fresh or thawed frozen)
2oz (60g) arugula
2oz (60g) baby spinach leaves
2 shallots, finely chopped
2 heirloom tomatoes, sliced

FOR THE VINAIGRETTE
1 tsp Dijon mustard
½ tsp ground cumin
Juice of ½ lime
3 tbsp ume plum vinegar
2 tbsp toasted sesame oil
2 tbsp canola or sunflower oil
Kosher salt and freshly ground black pepper
2 tsp toasted sesame seeds

> Preheat the oven to 375°F (190°C). Toss the bread cubes in the milk.
Spread on a baking sheet and toast in the oven until crisp, about
30 minutes. Cool.

> Cook the quinoa in boiling, lightly salted water in a small pan until just
tender, 15–20 minutes. Drain, rinse with cold water, and drain again.

> Place the corn kernels in a bowl. Add the arugula and spinach, the cooled
quinoa, and shallots. In a separate bowl, combine the mustard, cumin,
lime juice, and plum vinegar. Whisk together, then slowly whisk in the oils
until thick and smooth. Season with salt and pepper and add the toasted
sesame seeds. Drizzle the vinaigrette over the salad and toss gently.

> Arrange the sliced tomatoes on four plates. Gently pile the dressed salad
on top and garnish with the toasted rye croûtons.

APPLE AND BRIE QUESADILLAS

MAKES 8 /// PREP TIME: 20 MINUTES /// COOK TIME: ABOUT 24 MINUTES

2 Granny Smith apples
1 tbsp fresh lemon juice
About 1/4 cup olive oil
8 cups arugula
Kosher salt and freshly ground black pepper
8oz (225g) just-ripe Brie cheese
8 soft whole wheat tortillas

> Peel, core, and thinly slice the apples. Toss the apple slices with the lemon juice and 2 tbsp water to prevent browning.

> Heat 1 tbsp of the olive oil in a large skillet over medium heat. Add a few handfuls of arugula, sprinkle lightly with salt and pepper, and move around with tongs for a few seconds until the arugula is just wilted. Transfer to a bowl. Add a little more oil to the pan and continue to wilt the remaining arugula in the same way. Set aside.

> Drain the apple slices and pat dry on paper towels. Divide the Brie into eight portions and spread one portion onto a tortilla. On one half of the tortilla, arrange a few slices of apple and some wilted arugula. Fold over the other half of the tortilla and press together. Repeat with the remaining tortillas, Brie, apples, and arugula.

> Heat a little olive oil in the cleaned skillet. Put in a folded tortilla and cook over medium-high heat, pressing down with a spatula, until the base is brown and crisp. Turn over and brown the other side. Transfer the quesadilla to a cutting board. Cut into three or four wedges and keep warm. Repeat with the remaining quesadillas. Serve warm.

PEPPERED TUNA CARPACCIO

SERVES 4 /// PREP TIME: 10 MINUTES PLUS FREEZING /// COOK TIME: 0

8oz (225g) piece of fresh tuna loin
Extra virgin olive oil
2 tbsp coarsely crushed black peppercorns
Kosher or coarse sea salt
2 tbsp fresh Parmesan shavings
4 handfuls of arugula
Lemon wedges (optional)

> Brush the tuna with a little oil and roll in the peppercorns to coat completely (not the ends). Wrap tightly in plastic wrap to form a good round shape. Place in the freezer until firm but not frozen hard, 2–3 hours.

> Unwrap the tuna and slice as thinly as possible using a sharp knife. Arrange the slices in a circle on plates. Drizzle with olive oil and sprinkle with a few grains of kosher or sea salt. Scatter a few Parmesan shavings over each portion and put a pile of arugula in the center. If desired, serve with lemon wedges to squeeze over.

CALYPSO RICE SALAD

SERVES 4 /// PREP TIME: 15 MINUTES /// COOK TIME: 45–50 MINUTES

1 ½ cups wild rice

2 oranges

½ cup red currants, removed from their stems

1 red bell pepper, diced

4 green onions (scallions), cut in thin slices on the bias

1 small red onion, finely chopped

2 tbsp chopped fresh cilantro leaves

2 tbsp chopped fresh mint leaves

½ tsp ground coriander

¼ tsp cayenne

Juice of 1 small lime

3 tbsp extra virgin olive oil

1 tsp wild-blossom honey

Kosher salt and freshly ground black pepper

> Cook the wild rice in a pan of boiling salted water until just tender, 45–50 minutes. Drain, rinse with cold water, and drain again well. Tip the rice into a salad bowl.

> While the rice is cooking, peel the oranges, holding them over a bowl to catch the juice. Be sure to cut off all the white pith. Cut the flesh into sections, cutting down on either side of each membrane. Put the sections to one side. Squeeze all the peel, pith, and membranes over the bowl to collect the last of the juice, then discard. Set the juice aside.

> When the rice is ready, add the orange sections, red currants, red bell pepper, green and red onions, and herbs to the salad bowl.

> Add the spices, lime juice, oil, and honey to the orange juice and whisk to mix. Season to taste. Pour this dressing over the salad and toss gently. Serve at room temperature.

VINE-RIPE TOMATO AND BUFFALO MOZZARELLA WITH MARINATED BEETS AND ARUGULA SALAD

SERVES 4 /// PREP TIME: 10 MINUTES /// COOK TIME: 0

1 large or 4 small cooked beets, peeled and diced
1 small shallot, finely chopped
2 tbsp red wine vinegar
4 tbsp extra virgin olive oil
1 small bunch of arugula
4 small, fresh *mozzarella di bufala* (buffalo mozzarella) balls,
   drained and sliced
6 small vine-ripe tomatoes, quartered
Freshly ground black pepper

> Toss the beets and shallot with the wine vinegar and 2 tbsp of the olive oil. Add the arugula and toss gently again. Divide among four plates.

> Arrange the mozzarella slices and tomato quarters among the arugula and beets. Drizzle the remaining olive oil over and season well with fresh ground pepper.

// You can use the mini-mozzarella balls called "boconccini" if you prefer bite-sized pieces of cheese.

SEATTLE JIM'S PEA SALAD

SERVES 4 /// PREP TIME: 20 MINUTES /// COOK TIME: 5 MINUTES

4 slices of "uncured" applewood-smoked bacon
2 cups frozen English peas, thawed
1 small red onion, diced small
4oz (115g) snow peas, cut in slices on the bias
8oz (225g) can water chestnuts, drained and sliced
2 tbsp mayonnaise
2 tbsp sour cream or crème fraîche
1 tbsp apple cider vinegar
½ tsp minced garlic
4 tbsp chopped fresh dill
Kosher salt and freshly ground black pepper

> Broil or fry the bacon until crisp. Drain on paper towels, then break into small pieces.

> Dry the peas well on paper towels (if you don't do this, the salad will be too wet). Combine the peas, onion, snow peas, sliced water chestnuts, and bacon in a large bowl.

> In a small bowl, whisk together the mayonnaise, sour cream or crème fraîche, cider vinegar, garlic, and dill. Season to taste. Add to the salad and toss gently. Serve at room temperature.

// Jim Glass was one of my sous chefs at Google. He was the kamikaze of sous chefs. Now he's the European food director for Google. This is a delicious salad he made up.

CAULIFLOWER-ALMOND-GARLIC SOUP

SERVES 4–6 /// PREP TIME: 30 MINUTES /// COOK TIME: 27–37 MINUTES

1 red bell pepper
½ cup olive oil
1 cup sliced almonds
1 large, fresh garlic clove, peeled and very thinly sliced or chopped
½ tsp ground cumin
¼ tsp celery seed
⅛ tsp cayenne
1 small head cauliflower, trimmed and cut in small florets (about 12oz/350g)
1 cup canned crushed tomatoes
¼ cup sherry vinegar
4 cups good chicken stock
1 thick slice of sourdough loaf, crust removed, lightly toasted
   (center still chewy), and cubed
Kosher salt and freshly ground black pepper
Chopped fresh parsley leaves for garnish

> Char the bell pepper under the broiler (or hold it on the prongs of a
fork over a gas flame), turning occasionally, until the skin is blackened in
patches and blistering, about 15 minutes. Place in a plastic bag and let cool,
then scrape off the skin with a paring knife. Cut the pepper in half, remove
the stem and seeds, and roughly chop.

> Place a heavy-based pan over low heat. Add the olive oil and almonds
and let the oil heat up slowly, gently cooking the almonds until pale
golden, about 10 minutes (this method of cooking the almonds is called
confit). Add the garlic, cumin, and celery seed, and cook, stirring, for
2 minutes longer. Add the cayenne and cauliflower. Stir well, then cover
and cook until the cauliflower begins to soften, about 5 minutes.

> Add the canned tomatoes, bell pepper, and sherry vinegar, and cook, stirring, until the vinegar has almost all evaporated. Add the chicken stock. Bring to a boil, then reduce the heat and simmer until the cauliflower is soft, 20–30 minutes.

> Stir in the bread cubes, mixing well so the bread absorbs the oil and all of the toasty texture has dissolved. Purée the soup in a blender or food processor. Return to a clean pan and season to taste. Reheat before serving, garnished with chopped parsley.

ALMONDS ARE PACKED WITH VITAMIN E AND EARTHY, RICH FLAVOR. THEY CAN MOP UP DAMAGING FREE RADICALS AND KEEP YOUR BRAIN IN GREAT SHAPE.

BEET SALAD WITH SHEEP'S CHEESE AND OLIVES

SERVES 4 /// PREP TIME: 10 MINUTES /// COOK TIME: ABOUT 30 MINUTES

4–5 red beets, about 1lb (450g) in total, trimmed,
    taking care not to cut the skin
6 tbsp extra virgin olive oil
Juice of 2 small lemons
1 small garlic clove, crushed
Kosher salt and freshly ground black pepper
4 large handfuls of arugula
6oz (175g) *ricotta salata* or feta cheese, cubed
1/3 cup Kalamata olives, halved and pitted

> Steam the whole beets in a steamer, or covered metal colander over a pan of boiling water, until they are tender, about 30 minutes, depending on their size. When they are cool enough to handle, peel and cut in bite-sized chunks.

> Meanwhile, whisk together the olive oil, lemon juice, garlic, and a little salt and pepper.

> Toss the beets in half the dressing to coat them. Mound a generous handful of arugula on each of four plates. Arrange the beets, cheese, and olives over the arugula. Drizzle with the remaining dressing and add a grinding of pepper. Serve immediately.

// The tanginess from the cheese balances so well with the natural sweetness of beets. And the briny finish from the olives is a perfect counterpoint in this salad.

CELERY ROOT SALAD

SERVES 4 /// PREP TIME: 10 MINUTES PLUS CHILLING /// COOK TIME: 0

1 large head celery root (celeriac), about 1 1/2lb (675g)
1 tbsp fresh lemon juice
1/4 cup mayonnaise
1 tbsp extra virgin olive oil
2 tsp Champagne vinegar
1/2 tsp minced garlic
1 tbsp chopped dill pickles
1 tbsp finely chopped fresh dill
1 tbsp snipped fresh chives
2 tsp finely chopped fresh thyme leaves
1 green onion (scallion), thinly sliced
Kosher salt and freshly ground black pepper

> Peel the celery root and coarsely shred in a food processor or cut in thin matchsticks. Place immediately in a bowl of iced water with the lemon juice added (this will prevent the celery root from browning).

> Mix together the mayonnaise, oil, vinegar, and garlic in a mixing bowl. Stir in the pickles, dill, chives, and thyme. Drain the celery root and pat dry on paper towels, then add to the bowl along with the green onion. Mix gently to coat everything well. Add salt and pepper to taste. Refrigerate until ready to serve, to let the flavors develop.

// This is good with some cubes of cheese or sliced prosciutto for a light lunch.

SUMMER VEGAN SPINACH SALAD

SERVES 4 /// PREP TIME: 25 MINUTES /// COOK TIME: 0

1 cup cooked or canned garbanzos (chickpeas)
1 cup grape tomatoes, halved
¼ cup toasted pistachio nuts, slightly crushed
1 fresh mint sprig, torn in small pieces
9oz (250g) baby spinach leaves
1 cup pea shoots
1 avocado, peeled, pitted, and diced

FOR THE DRESSING
¼ cup cooked or canned garbanzos (chickpeas)
3 tbsp Dijon mustard
2 small shallots, finely chopped
1 garlic clove, preferably roasted
1 tsp pickled ginger
¼ tsp smoked paprika
1 tsp ground cumin
3 tbsp fresh orange juice
2 tbsp fresh lemon juice
2 tbsp tamari
¼ cup canola oil
3 tbsp extra virgin olive oil
Kosher salt and freshly ground black pepper

> First make the dressing. Place all the ingredients, except the oils and seasoning, in a blender and blend until fairly smooth. With the machine running, slowly add the canola oil, followed by the olive oil to make a dressing that is fairly thick and smooth. Season to taste.

> Arrange the salad ingredients in a bowl: Start with the garbanzos and tomatoes, then the pistachios and mint, then the spinach and pea shoots, and lastly the avocado. Trickle the dressing over, toss gently, and serve.

// If you want to take this to work for lunch, toss the avocado in lemon juice to prevent browning, and pack the dressing separately to trickle over the salad just before eating.

COLESLAW FOR LUNCH

SERVES 4–6 /// PREP TIME: 10 MINUTES /// COOK TIME: 0

2 tbsp pineapple juice or apple cider
4 tsp mayonnaise
2 tsp sour cream
1 tsp grated horseradish (or horseradish relish)
½ tsp white wine vinegar
Pinch of celery seed
Kosher salt and freshly ground black pepper
¼ head green cabbage, shredded
¼ small head red cabbage, shredded
2 carrots, shredded

FOR SERVING
Cubes of Montery Jack cheese, crumbled crisp-cooked "uncured"
  applewood-smoked bacon, and halved cherry tomatoes

> Whisk together the pineapple juice or apple cider, mayonnaise, sour
cream, horseradish, vinegar, and celery seed in a large bowl. Add salt
and pepper to taste.

> Add the shredded cabbages and carrots, and toss to coat everything
evenly. Store in a sealed container in the refrigerator until ready to use.

> To serve, top with cubes of cheese, some crumbled bacon, and halved
cherry tomatoes. Eat with whole grain bread.

CHINESE TOFU SALAD

SERVES 4 /// PREP TIME: 30 MINUTES /// COOK TIME: 0

1 head romaine, inner leaves only, cut across into ½in (1cm) pieces

½ small head napa cabbage, finely shredded

1 large red bell pepper, cut in thin strips

2 green onions (scallions), cut in thin slices on the bias

7oz (200g) package baked savory (or smoked) tofu,
   cut into ¼in (5mm) strips

2oz (60g) fresh sunflower sprouts or bean sprouts, rinsed and drained

¼ bunch of fresh cilantro leaves, coarsely chopped

2 tsp toasted sesame seeds

FOR THE WONTON CRISPS

9 wonton wrappers, thawed if frozen, cut in half and then across
   into ¼in (5mm) strips

Peanut oil for frying

Kosher salt

FOR THE DRESSING

¼ cup grapeseed oil

1 tbsp smooth peanut butter

1 tbsp apple cider vinegar

1 tbsp rice vinegar

1 tbsp soy sauce

1 tsp dried chili flakes

1 tbsp toasted sesame oil

2 tsp wild-blossom honey

1 garlic clove, crushed

1 tsp grated fresh ginger root

Freshly ground black pepper

> First make the wonton crisps. Heat ½in (1cm) peanut oil in a skillet
until the oil bubbles when you touch a chopstick to it (about 350°F/180°C).
Add the wonton strips, a handful at a time, and fry until they are brown
and crisp, about 15 seconds. Watch carefully to be sure they don't burn.
As they are done, use a slotted spoon to transfer them to a plate lined
with paper towels to drain. Sprinkle lightly with salt.

> Whisk together the grapeseed oil, peanut butter, vinegars, soy sauce, chili flakes, sesame oil, honey, garlic, and ginger in a mixing bowl until smooth. Add salt and pepper to taste.

> Just before serving, add the romaine, cabbage, bell pepper, green onions, tofu, sprouts, cilantro, and sesame seeds to the dressing and toss to coat everything evenly.

> Pile the salad onto four serving plates and top with the wonton crisps. Serve immediately.

LOBSTER BISQUE

SERVES 4 /// PREP TIME: 25 MINUTES /// COOK TIME: 1 1/4 HOURS

1 tbsp butter
1 shallot, chopped
1/4 cup long grain rice
1/2 tsp sweet paprika
Pinch of ground cinnamon
Juice of 1/2 lemon
A little milk
1 tbsp chopped fresh parsley

FOR THE SILKY LOBSTER STOCK
1 cooked Maine lobster
2 tbsp butter
1 carrot, diced
1 celery rib, diced
1 turnip, diced
2 shallots, diced
1 bay leaf
1/2 cup Sauvignon Blanc or other dry white wine
1 tbsp brandy
1/4 vanilla bean
1/8 tsp turmeric
2 fresh thyme sprigs
1 tbsp tomato paste
Kosher salt and white pepper

> First make the stock. Split the lobster in half and remove all the meat from the body and the claws. Finely chop the meat and reserve for the bisque. Melt the butter in heavy-based pan and sauté the carrot, celery, turnip, and shallots for 1 minute, stirring. Add the lobster carcass (the shells, head, and all) and the bay leaf, and sauté for 1 minute, stirring. Add the wine and boil for 1 minute. Pour the brandy into a soup ladle and ignite, then add to the pan along with the vanilla bean, turmeric, thyme, tomato paste, and 4 cups water. Stir well. Bring to a boil. Reduce the heat to medium, partially cover, and simmer for 1 hour. Strain the stock and season to taste.

> Rinse out the pan, and make the bisque. Melt the butter and sauté the shallot, stirring, until softened, about 1 minute. Stir in the rice and cook for 1 minute, stirring. Add the lobster stock, paprika, and cinnamon. Bring to a boil, stirring, then reduce the heat, partially cover, and simmer gently until the rice is really tender, about 10 minutes.

> Purée the mixture in a blender and pass through a strainer into a clean pan. Stir in the finely chopped lobster meat and the lemon juice. Thin with a little milk, if desired. Taste and add more seasoning, if necessary. Ladle into warm bowls and garnish with chopped parsley.

SUPER-SIMPLE AWESOME FISH TACOS

SERVES 1 /// PREP TIME: 5 MINUTES /// COOK TIME: ABOUT 6 MINUTES
3–4 frozen fish sticks (how do the square fish swim?)
1 soft flour or corn tortilla, or 2 crisp tortilla shells
4 tsp roasted habanero salsa or other chili salsa
¼ cup corn kernels (fresh or thawed frozen)
2 tbsp tartar sauce with jalapeños
A handful of shredded green or napa cabbage or lettuce

> Cook the fish sticks according to package directions. Warm the tortilla or shells according to package directions, too. Mix the salsa with the corn.

> Spread the tartar sauce over the tortilla or in the shells. Add the fish sticks, then the shredded cabbage or lettuce, and then the salsa-corn mix. You know what to do next. For soft tacos, roll up and eat. For crisp tacos, just munch!

// If you can't find tartar sauce with jalapeños, use ordinary tartar and add a few slices of jalapeño from a can or jar.

MIXED WHOLEGRAIN AND BERRY SALAD

SERVES 4 /// PREP TIME: 10 MINUTES /// COOK TIME: 15–20 MINUTES

1 cup wheat berries
½ cup kamut grains
¼ cup millet grains
¼ cup farro grains
1 head dinosaur kale (black cabbage), coarsely shredded
½ cup toasted sliced almonds
2 tbsp chopped candied ginger
4 tbsp dried blueberries or cranberries
4 tbsp extra virgin olive oil
1 tbsp white balsamic vinegar
½ tsp ground cinnamon
Kosher salt and freshly ground black pepper

> Cook the wheat berries and all the grains in a pan of boiling water until just tender but still nutty, 15–20 minutes. Drain, rinse with cold water, and drain again. Tip into a large salad bowl.

> Meanwhile, bring a pan of water to a boil, add the dinosaur kale, and blanch for 1 minute. Drain, rinse with cold water, and drain again. Add to the grains with the almonds, ginger, and berries.

> Whisk the oil, vinegar, and cinnamon together. Pour over the salad and toss gently. Season to taste and toss again. Serve at room temperature.

// This makes an amazing side dish for roasted poultry during the autumn or holidays. You can use cracked wheat instead of wheat berries, and brown rice instead of kamut.

THREE-BEAN SALAD

SERVES 4–6 /// PREP TIME: 15 MINUTES PLUS SOAKING ///
COOK TIME: 1 HOUR 10 MINUTES

4oz (115g) dried flageolet or navy beans, soaked in cold water overnight
  (or a 14oz/400g can flageolet or cannellini beans)
4oz (115g) dried red kidney beans, soaked in cold water overnight
  (or a 14oz/400g can)
2 fresh thyme sprigs
2 cups fresh shelled or frozen fava beans (or frozen Fordhook lima beans)
1 small onion, finely chopped
1 red bell pepper, finely chopped
4 Roma or plum tomatoes, seeded and diced, or 8 cherry or grape
  tomatoes, seeded and quartered
Tiny fresh mint sprigs for garnish

FOR THE VINAIGRETTE
¼ cup extra virgin olive oil
Juice of 1 lemon
¼ cup chopped fresh mint leaves
¼ cup chopped fresh flat-leaf (Italian) parsley leaves
Kosher salt and freshly ground black pepper

> Drain the soaked beans and place in separate pans with the thyme.
Cover with water, bring to a boil, and boil rapidly for 10 minutes, then
reduce the heat. Cover and simmer gently until tender, about 1 hour.
Drain, rinse with cold water, and drain again. (If using canned beans,
drain and rinse them. Chop the thyme and reserve.)

> Blanch the fava beans in boiling water for 2 minutes. Drain, rinse with
cold water, and drain again.

> Mix all the beans with the onion, bell pepper, and tomatoes, plus the
chopped thyme if using canned beans. Whisk the oil and lemon juice
together, and stir in the mint, parsley, and salt and pepper to taste. Pour
over the salad and toss gently. Check the seasoning, then refrigerate to
let the flavors develop. Serve garnished with tiny sprigs of mint.

CORN AND RADISH SALAD

SERVES 4 /// PREP TIME: 15 MINUTES /// COOK TIME: 0

3 tbsp fresh lime juice
2 tbsp extra virgin olive oil
1 tbsp finely chopped jalapeño chili (from a can or jar)
1/4 tsp kosher salt
Freshly ground black pepper
1 large bunch of red radishes, stems and leaves removed
4 ears of very fresh corn, shucked
2 green onions (scallions), cut in thin slices on the bias
A large handful of fresh cilantro leaves, coarsely chopped

> Whisk together the lime juice, olive oil, jalapeño, salt, and a few grinds of pepper in a bowl.

> Either simply slice the radishes, or cut them into 1/8in (3mm) slices, then stack them and cut across into 1/8in (3mm) wide matchsticks. Cut the kernels from the corn cobs.

> Add the corn, radishes, green onions, and cilantro to the dressing and toss to coat. Add more lime juice, jalapeño, salt, or pepper to taste.

// This salad is best if covered and stored for several hours or overnight in the refrigerator, to let the flavors develop.

ICED GAZPACHO

SERVES 4 /// PREP TIME: 25 MINUTES PLUS CHILLING /// COOK TIME: 6 MINUTES

2 red bell peppers
1lb (450g) ripe Roma or plum tomatoes
1 English cucumber, peeled
1 tbsp olive oil
1 shallot, finely chopped
1 garlic clove, peeled
1 tsp ground cumin
1 tsp paprika
1/2 tsp ground cinnamon
2 tbsp rice vinegar
1 tsp wild-blossom honey
1/2 tsp grated orange zest
2 tbsp snipped fresh chives
Kosher salt and freshly ground black pepper
Fresh mint and diced vegetables for garnish

> Char and peel the bell peppers (see page 160). Cut in half and remove the seeds. Put the tomatoes in a bowl, cover with boiling water, and leave for 30 seconds, then drain and cover with cold water. Drain again and remove the skins. Pass the tomatoes, then the cucumber, and then the bell pepper through the fine blade of a meat grinding attachment of an electric mixer to make a smooth purée. Alternatively, you can use a food processor.

> Heat the oil in a saucepan, add the shallot, garlic, and spices, and cook gently, stirring, until softened but not browned, about 1 minute. Add the tomato mixture along with the rice vinegar, honey, and orange zest. Bring to a boil, then reduce the heat as low as possible. Cover and simmer very gently for 5 minutes.

> Stir in the chives and season to taste. Let cool, then refrigerate. Serve in small soup cups, each garnished with two or three ice cubes, vegetables, and mint. As the ice melts, it thins the soup to just the right consistency.

// I grind the vegetables rather than using my food processor because I like the resulting texture. Plus, it doesn't create a red foamy liquid.

SILICON VALLEY SPLIT PEA SOUP

SERVES 6 /// PREP TIME: 15 MINUTES PLUS SOAKING /// COOK TIME: 3 HOURS

1 smoked ham hock, about 2 ¼ lb (1kg)
2 cups yellow split peas, soaked in plenty of cold water
  for several hours or overnight
2 carrots, cut in small dice
2 celery ribs, cut in small dice
1 large onion, finely chopped
1 tbsp tomato paste
1 large fresh thyme sprig
1 fresh oregano sprig
1 bay leaf
1 garlic clove, crushed
1 large russet (or other floury) potato, cut in small dice
14oz (400g) can crushed tomatoes
2 tbsp chopped fresh thyme leaves
Kosher salt and freshly ground black pepper

> Put the ham hock in a pot and cover with cold water. Bring to a boil, then throw away the water (this is to make sure the finished soup isn't too salty). Put the hock back in the pot and add 5 pints (2.5 liters) water along with the drained split peas, carrots, celery, and onion. Add the tomato paste, herb sprigs, bay leaf, and garlic. Bring to a boil. Reduce the heat to medium, partially cover, and simmer for 2 hours.

> Lift the hock out of the pot and set aside. Discard the herb sprigs and bay leaf. Add the potato and tomatoes to the pot. Bring back to a boil and simmer, partially covered, for 1 hour longer.

> Meanwhile, when the hock is cool enough to handle, pull all the meat off the bones, discarding the fat, skin, and tendons. Dice the meat and return to the soup. Stir in the chopped thyme and season to taste.

> Serve hot, with crusty sourdough bread.

COCOA CAPONATA ON CROSTINI

SERVES 4 /// PREP TIME: 20 MINUTES /// COOK TIME: 15 MINUTES

5 tbsp olive oil
2 red bell peppers, diced
2 yellow bell peppers, diced
1 small onion, chopped
2 garlic cloves, thinly sliced
1/2 cup pine nuts, toasted
1/4 cup golden raisins
1 tbsp unsweetened cocoa powder
1/4 cup unrefined light brown sugar
1/4 cup red wine vinegar
1/4 cup balsamic vinegar
2oz (60g) can anchovies, drained and chopped
1/2 cup Kalamata olives, pitted and chopped
1 tsp dried chili flakes (or more to taste)
2 tbsp chopped fresh flat-leaf (Italian) parsley leaves
Kosher salt and freshly ground black pepper
8 slices of French bread, cut on the bias

> Heat 1 tbsp of the oil in a large pan and sauté the bell peppers with the onion for 3 minutes, stirring. Add the garlic, pine nuts, golden raisins, cocoa powder, and sugar. Blend in the vinegars, then reduce the heat and cover. Simmer gently until most of the liquid has evaporated and the peppers are glazed and just tender, about 15 minutes. Let cool slightly, then stir in the anchovies, olives, chili flakes, parsley, and seasoning to taste.

> Heat the remaining olive oil in a skillet and sauté the French bread slices until golden on both sides. Drain on paper towels. Pile the warm caponata on the crostini and serve.

// You can rub the crostini with a cut garlic clove before topping with the caponata. It also goes great with broiled or grilled chicken or fish.

DUCK AND SHRIMP DIM SUM

MAKES 12 /// PREP TIME: 45 MINUTES /// COOK TIME: 5 MINUTES

1 small jicama, peeled and cut in chunks
1 small carrot, peeled
2 green onions (scallions), trimmed
1/4 cup peeled rock shrimp
1 skinless duck breast, cut in pieces
1/4 cup pancetta (Italian bacon), cut in pieces
1 tsp minced ginger
1 tsp minced garlic
1 tbsp black sesame seeds
1 tbsp black or balsamic vinegar
1/2 tsp toasted sesame oil
1 tbsp tamari
12 outer bok choy leaves (from 2–3 heads)
12 thin slices of fresh, hot red chili
Sweet chili dipping sauce for serving

> With the machine of a food processor running, drop the jicama, carrot, and green onions into the bowl, followed by the shrimp, duck, and pancetta. When finely minced, add the remaining ingredients, except the bok choy, chili, and dipping sauce, and pulse to mix.

> Blanch the bok choy leaves in boiling water for 45 seconds. Drain, rinse with cold water, and drain again.

> Take one leaf at a time and gently spread out on paper towels. Pat dry. Put a small spoonful of the filling on the green part of the leaf. Fold in the green edges, then wrap the white stem up and over, then around underneath the filling, so the package is sitting in the cup of the white stem. If necessary, gently straighten out the sides of the green so the filling is almost covered.

> Place the dim sum in a bamboo or other steamer. Cover and steam for 5 minutes.

> Serve in Asian soup spoons, with a small amount of sweet chili dipping sauce in the bottom of each spoon and garnished with the chili slices. Alternatively, arrange the dim sum on a platter, garnish each with a slice of chili, and put a small bowl of dipping sauce in the center.

// These make a great snack, but you could also serve them as an appetizer, or as a light lunch with a crisp bean sprout and shredded vegetable salad (or some rice noodles tossed in soy sauce). Use the hearts of the bok choy, shredded, in the salad.

BARLEY-CORN SALAD

SERVES 4 /// PREP TIME: 15 MINUTES /// COOK TIME: 40 MINUTES

⅓ cup pearl barley
Kosher salt and freshly ground black pepper
1 small red bell pepper
2 tbsp tamari
2 tbsp ume plum vinegar
1 tbsp soy oil
2 tsp toasted sesame oil
2 tsp finely chopped pickled ginger
2 tsp black sesame seeds
3 green onions (scallions), cut in thin slices on the bias
1 large or 2 small ears of corn

> Bring ¾ cup water with ¼ tsp kosher salt to a boil. Add the pearl barley and cook until tender and most of the liquid has been absorbed, about 40 minutes. Leave, covered, off the heat to absorb any remaining liquid.

> Meanwhile, char the pepper under the broiler (or hold it on the prongs of a fork over a gas flame), turning occasionally, until the skin is blackened in patches and blistering, about 15 minutes. Place it in a plastic bag and let cool. Scrape off the skin with a paring knife. Cut in half, remove the stem and seeds, and cut in ½in (1cm) dice.

> In a serving bowl, whisk together the tamari, vinegar, and oils. Stir in the ginger and sesame seeds. Add the green onions and diced bell pepper. Toss to coat. Cut the kernels off the corn cobs and add to the bowl along with the pearl barley. Toss again. Add pepper to taste. Serve the salad warm or at room temperature.

// These are two of my favorites—cooked pearl barley and fresh corn kernels from the cob. The corn can be cooked, if you prefer, but I like the way it tastes raw in contrast to the cooked barley.

SANTA BARBARA SALAD

SERVES 1 /// PREP TIME: 15 MINUTES /// COOK TIME: 0
A large handful of baby spinach leaves, about 1oz (30g)
A large handful of arugula, about 1oz (30g)
1 small carrot, thinly sliced
4 button mushrooms, sliced
1 small beet, shredded
3 cherry tomatoes, halved
2 tsp toasted pumpkin seeds

FOR THE VINAIGRETTE
½ small shallot, finely chopped
1 tbsp extra virgin olive oil
1 tsp red wine vinegar
¼ tsp Dijon mustard
1 tsp chopped fresh thyme leaves
¼ tsp ground cumin
Kosher salt and freshly ground black pepper

> Whisk the vinaigrette ingredients together in a salad bowl. Add all
the salad ingredients, except the pumpkin seeds, and toss gently. Scatter
the pumpkin seeds over and serve.

DEREK, MY SURFER-COOK AT GOOGLE, CAME UP WITH THIS. IT HAS ALL THE GOOD THINGS ABOUT BEING A CALIFORNIAN.

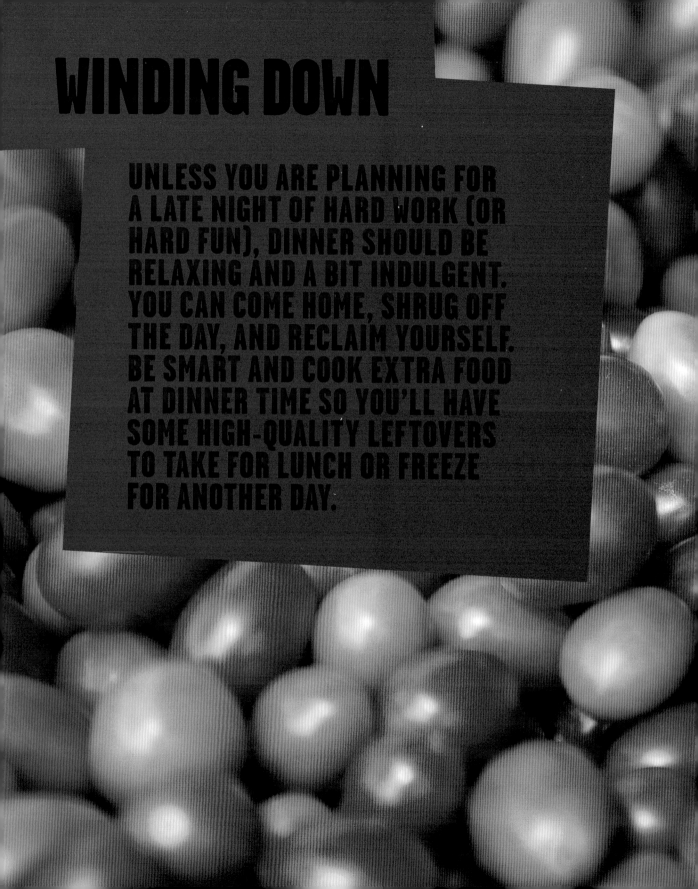

WINDING DOWN

UNLESS YOU ARE PLANNING FOR A LATE NIGHT OF HARD WORK (OR HARD FUN), DINNER SHOULD BE RELAXING AND A BIT INDULGENT. YOU CAN COME HOME, SHRUG OFF THE DAY, AND RECLAIM YOURSELF. BE SMART AND COOK EXTRA FOOD AT DINNER TIME SO YOU'LL HAVE SOME HIGH-QUALITY LEFTOVERS TO TAKE FOR LUNCH OR FREEZE FOR ANOTHER DAY.

SEARED SOUTHWESTERN AHI TUNA TORNADOES

SERVES 4 /// PREP TIME: 10 MINUTES /// COOK TIME: 3–4 MINUTES

1lb (450g) piece *ahi* (yellowfin) tuna loin (or 4 small, thick tuna steaks)
2 tbsp canola oil
2 tbsp Southwestern Spice Rub (see page 63)
½ cup mayonnaise
Juice of 1 lime
1 avocado, peeled, pitted, and mashed
1 fresh serrano chili, seeded and finely chopped
1 shallot, finely chopped
8 soft flour tortillas
1 small jicama, shredded
1 large carrot, shredded
½ small head napa cabbage, shredded
A large handful of fresh cilantro leaves

> Brush the tuna all over with the oil, then season with the spice rub. Heat a ridged cast-iron grill pan and sear the tuna on all sides for 3–4 minutes; the fish should still be rare in the center. Remove from the pan and let cool, then cut in thin slices.

> Mix the mayonnaise with the lime juice, avocado, chili, and shallot.

> Warm the tortillas. Lay each one on a piece of wax paper or a napkin. Spread the mayonnaise over the tortillas, then add some jicama, then carrot, and then cabbage. Add the sliced tuna and a few cilantro leaves.

> At the bottom of each tortilla, fold over one side at an extreme angle, then continue to wrap into a cone shape.

// This is a little play on sushi and southwestern foods together: I replaced the nori seaweed roll with a flour tortilla and used a spicy avocado mayonnaise instead of rice.

LAMB KORMA

SERVES 4 /// PREP TIME: 40 MINUTES PLUS MARINATING /// COOK TIME: 1 ½–2 HOURS

2 large onions
1in (2.5cm) piece of fresh ginger root, grated
2 garlic cloves, roughly chopped
1 tsp coriander seeds, roughly crushed
1 tsp ground cumin
4 cardamom pods, split and seeds removed
½ tsp kosher salt
½ tsp dried chili flakes
1 ½lb (675g) lean boneless lamb, diced
2 tbsp ghee
2 tbsp tomato paste
½ cup plain yogurt
A few fresh cilantro leaves, torn, for garnish

> Chop one onion; halve and slice the other. Put the chopped onion in
a mortar (or small bowl) and add the ginger, garlic, coriander, cumin,
cardamom seeds, salt, and chili flakes. Pound the mixture to a paste with
a pestle or the end of a rolling pin. Alternatively, use an immersion blender.

> Put the lamb in a bowl and add the spice paste. Mix well, then let
marinate in a cool place or the refrigerator for at least 1 hour.

> Heat the ghee in a pan, add the sliced onion, and sauté for 2 minutes,
stirring. Add the lamb and cook, stirring, until browned all over, about
5 minutes. Add the tomato paste and yogurt. Bring to a boil, stirring well,
then reduce the heat, cover, and simmer gently, stirring occasionally, until
the lamb is really tender and bathed in a rich sauce, 1 ½–2 hours.

> Spoon into a serving dish and garnish with cilantro. Serve with rice,
cucumber raita (thick plain yogurt mixed with fresh mint, garlic, and finely
diced English cucumber), and Indian relishes.

SEA BASS AND SCALLOPS WITH MINTY PEA SAUCE

SERVES 2 /// PREP TIME: 25 MINUTES /// COOK TIME: 18–20 MINUTES

1 carrot, diced

1 yellow or orange bell pepper, diced

1 large tomato, diced

1 cup drained, canned cannellini
    beans

Kosher salt and white pepper

2 tbsp olive oil

1 Yukon Gold potato (or other all-
    purpose variety), peeled and sliced

2 small sea bass fillets, about 4oz
    (115g) each, cut in half

4 diver sea scallops

Fresh chive stems for garnish

FOR THE MINTY PEA SAUCE

2 tsp olive oil

1 small shallot, finely chopped

½ tsp minced garlic

2 cups frozen English peas, thawed

2 tbsp chopped fresh mint leaves

2 cups chicken or vegetable stock

> First make the pea sauce. Heat the olive oil in a saucepan and sauté the shallot very gently, stirring, until soft but not brown, about 1 minute. Add the garlic, peas, mint, and half the stock. Bring to a boil, then reduce the heat and simmer until the peas are tender, about 5 minutes. Purée in a blender, adding enough of the remaining stock to give a thick but pourable consistency. Return to the pan and set aside.

> While the peas are simmering, blanch the carrot in boiling water for 3 minutes; drain, rinse with cold water, and drain again. Return to the pan and mix in the bell pepper, tomato, and beans. Season to taste. Set aside.

> Heat 1 tbsp of the olive oil in a skillet and fry the potato slices until golden on both sides and cooked through, about 6 minutes. Drain on paper towels and keep warm. Wipe out the skillet.

> Season the fish fillets and scallops. Heat the remaining 1 tbsp olive oil in the skillet until very hot but not smoking. Sauté the sea bass, skin-side down, with the scallops until golden, 1–2 minutes. Gently turn the fish and scallops over and quickly sear the other sides for 1–2 minutes longer. Take care not to overcook the fish. Remove from the pan and keep warm.

> Reheat the pea sauce, and toss the bean mixture over a gentle heat to warm through. Spoon the pea sauce onto deep, warm plates, spreading it out to a large pool. Add the potato slices. Place two pieces of sea bass, skin-side down, and two scallops on top of each pool. Spoon the vegetable mixture alongside and garnish with chives.

BUTTERNUT CHILIJACK

SERVES 4 /// PREP TIME: 20 MINUTES /// COOK TIME: 25–30 MINUTES

2 butternut squashes, peeled, seeded, and diced
2 red onions, diced
1/4 cup sliced jalapeño chilies (from a can or jar)
1 tbsp mild chili powder
1/4 tsp cayenne (optional)
Kosher salt and freshly ground black pepper
2 tbsp grapeseed oil
2 tomatoes, diced, or 1 cup drained, canned crushed tomatoes
2 cups frozen corn kernels, thawed
2 cups shredded Monterey Jack cheese
A handful of fresh cilantro leaves, torn in pieces

> Preheat the oven to 375°F (190°C). Combine the squash, onions, and chilies in a roasting pan and season with the chili powder, cayenne, salt, and pepper. Drizzle the grapeseed oil over and toss well. Roast until just tender but still with some texture, 25–30 minutes.

> Remove from the oven and tip into a large bowl. Add the tomatoes, corn, Monterey jack cheese, and cilantro. Mix gently until the cheese begins to melt. Serve warm.

THIS IS A SLAMMING DISH. IT WAS BORN FROM LEFTOVERS AND THE NEED TO COME UP WITH A VEGETARIAN DISH ON THE FLY AT GOOGLE.

GOAN PORK

SERVES 4 /// PREP TIME: 20 MINUTES PLUS MARINATING /// COOK TIME: 1 HOUR

4 fresh red chilies (serranos work well), seeds left in if you dare
1/4 cup rice vinegar
1/4 cup black vinegar
3 tbsp cumin seeds
2 tbsp black mustard seeds
1 tsp turmeric
1 tsp freshly ground black pepper
1/2 tsp ground cardamom
1/2 tsp ground cloves
Pinch of grated nutmeg (or more, depending on how much you like nutmeg)
1 large onion, roughly chopped
2 large garlic cloves, peeled
1in (2.5cm) piece of fresh ginger root, peeled
6 tbsp canola oil
1 1/2 tbsp palm sugar or unrefined light brown sugar
1 tsp kosher salt
3/4 cup apple cider vinegar
2lb (900g) boneless pork shoulder or butt, cut into 1 1/2in (4cm) cubes
3 bay leaves
Fresh bay leaves for garnish

> Soak the chilies in the mixed rice and black vinegars for at least 30 minutes. Heat a sauté pan and toast the cumin and mustard seeds for 1 minute, stirring. Tip into a food processor and add the remaining spices, the onion, garlic, ginger, and chilies with their soaking vinegar. Add 1 1/2 tbsp of the canola oil, the sugar, salt, and cider vinegar. Purée to a smooth paste.

> Put the diced pork in a container with a sealable lid. Stir in the curry paste, cover, and let marinate in the refrigerator overnight.

> The next day, when you are ready to cook this fiery pork dish, heat the remaining oil in a heavy-based pan. Remove the pork from the marinade and braise over medium heat, stirring, for 5 minutes. Add the bay leaves

and the marinade, partially cover, and continue to cook on low heat, stirring occasionally, until the pork is tender and bathed in sauce, about 1 hour. During cooking, add water as needed to keep the sauce rich and thick.

> Discard the bay leaves. Taste and adjust the seasoning. Garnish with fresh bay leaves and serve with plenty of naan breads and rice.

ITALIAN CHICKEN WITH TOMATOES AND PEPPERS

SERVES 4 /// PREP TIME: 30 MINUTES /// COOK TIME: 1 HOUR

3lb (1.35kg) chicken, cut in 8 pieces
Kosher salt and freshly ground black pepper
2 tbsp olive oil
2 yellow bell peppers, diced
2 carrots, diced
1 large onion, finely chopped
1 large garlic clove, finely chopped
2 cups red wine
14oz (400g) can crushed tomatoes
¼ cup tomato paste
2 tbsp chopped fresh oregano leaves
2 tbsp chopped fresh basil leaves

> Season the chicken. Heat the oil in a heavy-based pan. Add the chicken and brown all over. Remove from the pan. Add the peppers and carrots, and sauté until they get a little color, about 2 minutes. Add the onion and sauté for 1 more minute. Add the garlic and wine, and boil, stirring, until reduced by half. Add the tomatoes and tomato paste. Season to taste.

> Return the chicken to the pan. Bring to a boil, then reduce the heat, cover, and simmer very gently until the chicken is really tender and the sauce is rich and thick, about 1 hour. During cooking, add a little water as necessary to prevent the sauce from becoming too concentrated.

> Add the herbs for the last 5 minutes of the cooking time. Taste and add more seasoning, if necessary. Serve with pasta or potato gnocchi.

// Toward the end of the cooking time, do not stir the chicken pieces or move them around excessively, or the meat will fall off the bone and the presentation will be spoiled.

JAPANESE BEEF CURRY

SERVES 4 /// PREP TIME: 30 MINUTES /// COOK TIME: 2 HOURS

2lb (900g) lean stewing steak, such as chuck, cut into 1 ½in (4cm) cubes
3 tbsp tamari
3 tbsp black or balsamic vinegar
4 tbsp rice or sunflower oil
3 tbsp all-purpose flour
2 shallots, chopped
1 leek, white part only, sliced
1 garlic clove, thinly sliced
½in (1cm) piece of fresh ginger root, grated
1 carrot, sliced
1 small head celery root (celeriac), diced
½ tsp turmeric
1 tsp coarsely ground black pepper
½ tbsp paprika
⅛ tsp ground cloves
1 tsp ground coriander
½ cup spring water
1 tbsp red miso paste
2 green onions (scallions), chopped
1 tbsp toasted sesame seeds

> Toss the beef in 1 tbsp each of the tamari and vinegar. Heat 3 tbsp of the oil in a large, heavy-based pan. Sprinkle in the flour and cook until slightly browned, about 1 minute. Add the beef and sauté, stirring, until browned, about 5 minutes. Remove the beef from pan.

> Add the remaining 1 tbsp oil and heat it, then sauté the shallots, leek, garlic, and ginger for 2 minutes. Add the carrot, celery root, and spices, and cook for 30 seconds, stirring. Add the remaining 2 tbsp vinegar.

> When the vinegar has almost all evaporated, return the beef to the pan. Stir well, then add the spring water and miso. Bring to a boil. Reduce the heat, partially cover, and simmer very gently until the meat and vegetables are very tender, about 2 hours. Season with the remaining tamari. Serve spooned over rice, garnished with the green onions and sesame seeds.

LAMB BURGERS WITH TZATZIKI SAUCE

SERVES 4 /// PREP TIME: 15 MINUTES PLUS CHILLING /// COOK TIME: 6–8 MINUTES

1lb (450g) good-quality ground lamb
1 tsp minced garlic
½ tsp ground cloves
1 tsp ground cumin
Kosher salt and freshly ground black pepper
1 tbsp olive oil
4 artisan-style hard rolls
4 small handfuls of baby spinach leaves

FOR THE MARINATED ONIONS
½ red onion, thinly sliced
1 tbsp red wine vinegar
1 tsp unrefined light brown sugar

FOR THE SAUCE
2in (5cm) piece of English cucumber, coarsely grated
¼ cup Greek-style plain yogurt
¼ tsp minced garlic
2 tbsp chopped fresh mint leaves

> Put the lamb in a bowl and add the garlic, cloves, cumin, and plenty of freshly ground black pepper. Mix with your hands until well combined, then shape into four burgers. Chill until ready to cook.

> Mix the red onion with the vinegar and sugar. Let marinate while you prepare the sauce. Squeeze the cucumber to remove excess moisture, then mix with the yogurt, garlic, mint, and a little salt and pepper. Chill.

> When ready to eat, heat a ridged cast-iron grill pan. Sprinkle the burgers with a little kosher salt and brush with olive oil. Cook the burgers until browned and cooked through, 3–4 minutes on each side.

> Meanwhile, split the rolls and toast them. When the burgers are cooked, assemble your creation with baby spinach leaves, tzatziki sauce, and the drained marinated onions.

BROILED SALMON-PESTO-TOMATO BUNDLES

SERVES 2 /// PREP TIME: 25 MINUTES /// COOK TIME: 25 MINUTES

10 thin asparagus spears
2 cups cooked long grain rice
2 pieces of wild salmon fillet, about 4oz (115g) each
Kosher salt and freshly ground black pepper
2 tbsp olive oil
2 vine-ripe tomatoes, halved
2 tbsp fresh bread crumbs
2 tbsp pesto (from a jar or refrigerated tub)
2 lemon wedges

> Blanch the asparagus in boiling water for 2 minutes. Drain, rinse with cold water, and drain again. Preheat the broiler.

> Lay two sheets of foil on the broiler rack and top each with a piece of parchment paper. Put a cup of rice in the center of each piece of paper. Lay five asparagus spears on each mound of rice and top with a salmon fillet. Season with salt and pepper, and drizzle with the olive oil. Place the tomatoes on the fish. Mix the bread crumbs and pesto together and spoon this over the tomatoes.

> Place under the broiler, about 5in (12.5cm) from the heat, and cook for 5 minutes. Remove from the heat. Turn off the broiler and switch the oven on to 375°F (190°C).

> Carefully pull up all four sides of each sheet of foil over the filling and gently tuck the edges together to create a teepee-shaped bundle. Make sure the edges of each bundle are sealed tightly. Return to the oven and cook for 20 minutes longer.

> Place the bundles on plates, open up the foil, and serve with wedges of lemon to squeeze over.

LINGUINE WITH PORTUGUESE CLAM SAUCE

SERVES 4 /// PREP TIME: 15 MINUTES /// COOK TIME: 22 MINUTES

1lb (450g) fresh clams, scrubbed and any open ones discarded
   (or a 10oz/300g can clams)
1 tsp dried chili flakes
2 cups V8 vegetable juice
Juice of 1/2 lemon
1 tsp dried oregano
1 garlic clove, crushed
12oz (350g) linguine
1 tbsp butter
Kosher salt and freshly ground black pepper

> If using fresh clams, put them in a large pan with about 1/2in (1cm)
boiling water. Cover and steam for 5 minutes, shaking the pan occasionally.
Drain, reserving 1 cup of the cooking liquor. Discard any clams that have
not opened. (If using canned clams, drain them and reserve the juice.)

> Put the chili flakes in a pan and toast gently, stirring, until fragrant,
about 1 minute. Take care not to burn them. Add the vegetable juice and
clam cooking liquor (or juice from the can). Bring to a boil and boil rapidly
until reduced by half, about 10 minutes. Add the lemon juice and oregano,
and simmer for 5 minutes longer. Stir in the garlic.

> While the sauce is simmering, cook the linguine according to package
directions. Drain the pasta and return to its pot. Stir in the clam sauce
and butter. Add the clams. Toss gently over low heat for 1 minute. Taste
for salt—it should taste like the ocean—and then serve.

// You could use Clamato juice instead of V8. With canned clams, the
prep time will be only 5 minutes.

MEXICAN CHICKEN AND CAPER STEW

SERVES 4–6 /// PREP TIME: 25 MINUTES /// COOK TIME: 40 MINUTES

1 red bell pepper
8 skinless, boneless chicken thighs, diced
1 cup chicken stock
4 potatoes, diced
1 onion, roughly chopped
2 tomatoes, chopped
2 tbsp capers, roughly chopped
2 cups pineapple juice
4 tbsp dry white wine
1 bay leaf
1 tsp ground cumin
3/4 tsp dried oregano
Kosher salt and freshly ground black pepper
2 tbsp roughly chopped fresh cilantro leaves

> Char the bell pepper under the broiler (or hold it on the prongs of a fork over a gas flame), turning occasionally, until the skin is blackened in patches and blistering, about 15 minutes. Place in a plastic bag and let cool, then scrape off the skin with a paring knife. Cut the pepper in half, remove the stem and seeds, and cut in dice.

> Place the chicken in a heavy-based pan with the chicken stock. Bring to a boil, then reduce the heat and simmer for 10 minutes. Add the diced pepper and all the remaining ingredients, except the cilantro, and bring back to a boil. Reduce the heat again and simmer until the chicken and potatoes are tender, about 30 minutes.

> Taste and add more seasoning, if necessary. Discard the bay leaf, garnish with the cilantro, and serve with plain rice.

// This is also good with 2 tbsp sliced jalapeños (from a can or jar) added with the capers.

FILET MIGNON WITH MELTED FRISÉE

SERVES 2 /// PREP TIME: 30 MINUTES /// COOK TIME: 25 MINUTES

6–8 small fingerling potatoes, scrubbed
2 baby carrots, scrubbed
5 tbsp olive oil
Kosher salt and freshly ground black pepper
2 filet mignon steaks, about 4oz (115g) each, trimmed
1 small head frisée, halved (or 2 wedges of a larger head)
2 shallots, finely chopped
1 tsp minced garlic
1 cup frozen English peas, thawed
4 tsp Banyuls or sherry vinegar
3 tbsp white miso broth
1 tbsp unsalted butter
1 tbsp chopped fresh basil leaves

> Preheat the broiler. Place the potatoes and carrots on a large sheet
of foil. Drizzle with 2 tbsp of the olive oil, season with salt and pepper,
and add 2 tbsp water. Bring the corners of the foil together and fold over
to form a sealed package. Place on the broiler rack and cook under the
broiler, about 5in (12.5cm) from the heat, for 25 minutes.

> Brush the steaks with a little oil. When the potato package has been
cooking for 15 minutes, add the steaks to the broiler rack and cook to the
desired degree of doneness (2–6 minutes on each side). Remove from the
broiler and keep hot. Place the frisée on the broiler rack and broil until
it wilts and is lightly caramelized on the outside, 3–5 minutes.

> Meanwhile, heat the remaining oil in a sauté pan, add the shallots, and
sauté, stirring, until just turning golden, about 2 minutes. Add the garlic
and peas, and stir well. Add the vinegar and bubble until it has almost
all evaporated, then stir in the miso broth, butter, and basil.

> Open the foil package. Place three or four potatoes in the center of each
plate, set a steak on the potatoes, and top with the melted frisée. Spoon
the pea mixture over and around, and rest a carrot gently next to each
steak with its tip pointing up. Serve immediately.

ORANGE FIRE CHICKEN

SERVES 4 /// PREP TIME: 7 MINUTES /// COOK TIME: 2 HOURS

4–6 skinless, boneless chicken breast halves, cut in chunks

1/4 tsp habanero chili powder

Finely grated zest of 1/2 orange

3 tbsp tomato purée

1 tbsp tomato paste

1/4 tsp ground cinnamon

2 tsp shredded pickled ginger

1 tsp ground coriander

1/4 tsp sweet smoked paprika

2 cups Sauvignon Blanc or other dry white wine

1 bay leaf

2 tsp toasted sesame seeds

1 1/2 tbsp unrefined light brown sugar

1 tsp minced garlic

4 tbsp tamari

Kosher salt and freshly ground black pepper

1 tbsp chopped fresh parsley

> Put all the ingredients, except the parsley, in an enameled cast-iron pot and stir well. Bring to a boil. Reduce the heat to as low as possible, cover, and simmer very gently for 1 3/4 hours.

> Remove the lid of the pot, turn up the heat slightly, and simmer, stirring occasionally, until the sauce has reduced and thickened, about 15 minutes. Taste and add more seasoning, if necessary. Serve over couscous, quinoa, or rice, garnished with chopped parsley.

// Cast iron is a solid conductor of heat and retains its own heat really well, so you need to cook over a very low temperature.

SNAPPER IN A YOGURT COAT

SERVES 4 /// PREP TIME: 30 MINUTES PLUS SOAKING AND MARINATING ///
COOK TIME: 20 MINUTES

1 whole red snapper (or striped
   bass or white bass), about
   3lb (1.35kg), cleaned and scaled,
   fins removed
Freshly ground black pepper
Chopped fresh flat-leaf (Italian)
   parsley
Fresh lemon juice
4 super-ripe tomatoes, sliced

FOR THE YOGURT COAT
¼ cup raisins
3 tbsp boiling water
2 cups thick, whole-milk plain yogurt
1 ½ tsp ground cumin
1 tsp turmeric
1 tsp ground ginger
½ tsp ground cinnamon
1 tsp white pepper
3 tbsp fresh lemon juice
½ tsp garlic purée
1 tsp fish sauce
1 tbsp white sesame seeds

> First make the yogurt coat. Soak the raisins in the boiling water until
plumped and soft, about 30 minutes. Place in a food processor, add the
rest of the coat ingredients, and blend until smooth.

> Make a few slanted cuts along the sides of the fish, about 1in (2.5cm)
long. Cover the fish in the yogurt coat and refrigerate for 2–4 hours.

> Preheat the broiler. Place the fish in a foil-lined broiler pan. Spoon
enough of the yogurt marinade over to cover the fish and grind some
pepper over it. Broil, about 5in (12.5cm) from the heat, for 10 minutes. The
coating on the fish will go from a yellowish brown to golden brown, and
then to dark brown very fast. Watch carefully to be sure it doesn't burn.

> Turn the fish over, coat with more of the yogurt marinade, and grind
more pepper over. Broil for 10 minutes longer. To make sure it doesn't
get too brown, turn off the broiler just as the color is turning brown.

> Let the fish rest for a few moments, then set it on a bed of chopped
parsley on a platter. Squeeze some lemon juice over the fish and layer
sliced tomatoes on top. Serve with couscous and steamed greens.

SEITAN OR QUORN WELLINGTONS

SERVES 4 /// PREP TIME: 20 MINUTES PLUS COOLING /// COOK TIME: 15–20 MINUTES

2 tbsp unsalted butter
2 shallots, finely chopped
8oz (225g) button mushrooms, thinly sliced
2 tbsp chopped fresh thyme
1 cup good drinking red wine
½ tsp minced garlic
Kosher salt and freshly ground black pepper
4 large sheets phyllo pastry
1 tbsp sunflower oil
8 bite-sized pieces of seitan or 4 Quorn cutlets
Fresh parsley sprigs for garnish

> Melt the butter in a sauté pan and sauté the shallots, stirring, until softened, about 1 minute. Add the mushrooms and stir until they begin to soften. Add the thyme, wine, garlic, and a little salt and pepper. Simmer, stirring, until the wine has almost evaporated but the mixture is still moist. Let cool.

> Preheat the oven to 375°F (190°C). Brush the sheets of phyllo with a little oil and fold in half to form squares. Brush lightly with oil again. Spoon the mushroom mixture onto the center of the squares. Top with either two pieces of seitan or a Quorn cutlet. Season with salt and pepper. Fold the pastry over the filling to form sealed packages. Place sealed-side down on a lightly oiled baking sheet. Brush the packages with a little oil.

> Bake until crisp and golden, 15–20 minutes. Cut the wellingtons in half and arrange on serving plates. Garnish with sprigs of parsley and serve with creamed potatoes and a crisp green salad.

ORANGE-MARINATED CHICKEN WITH CARROT-HARISSA PASTA

SERVES 4 /// PREP TIME: 20 MINUTES PLUS MARINATING ///
COOK TIME: ABOUT 20 MINUTES

4 skinless, boneless chicken breast halves
Finely grated zest and juice of 1 orange
2 tsp wild-blossom honey
1 tbsp olive oil
1 tsp minced garlic
Kosher salt and freshly ground black pepper
12oz (350g) fusilli pasta

FOR THE SAUCE
1 tsp caraway seeds
1/2 tsp cumin seeds
1 tsp dried chili flakes
1 tbsp pickled ginger, squeezed dry and finely chopped
1 tsp minced garlic
2 cups carrot juice (preferably freshly made)
Finely grated zest of 1 orange
14oz (400g) can garbanzos (chickpeas), drained
1 tbsp butter
4 handfuls of baby spinach leaves

> Make several slashes in each chicken breast, so the marinade flavors will soak in. Lay the chicken in a shallow dish in a single layer. Whisk the orange zest and juice with the honey, oil, garlic, and a little salt and pepper. Pour this over the chicken. Turn to coat completely, then let marinate in a cool place or the refrigerator for at least 1 hour.

> Toast the caraway and cumin seeds with the chili flakes in a pan until they become fragrant, about 2 minutes. Crush in a clean coffee grinder or mortar and pestle (or in a bowl with the end of a rolling pin). Return to the pan and add the ginger, garlic, carrot juice, and orange zest. Bring to a boil. Reduce the heat and simmer gently until reduced by half, about 10 minutes.

> Add the garbanzos and butter, and simmer for 5 minutes longer. Throw the spinach into the pan, cover, and cook until wilted, about 2 minutes. Season to taste.

> While the sauce is simmering, cook the pasta according to package directions; drain and return to the pot. At the same time, heat a ridged cast-iron grill pan, drain the chicken (reserve the marinade), and pan-grill until lightly browned and cooked through, 3–4 minutes on each side.

> Add the garbanzo sauce to the pasta and toss well. Pour any remaining marinade and 2–3 tbsp water into the grill pan and bubble for a few seconds, stirring well.

> Pile the pasta on warm plates and put a piece of chicken alongside the pasta. Spoon the juices over and serve.

// For the pasta sauce, you can cheat and use 2 tbsp ready-made harissa paste mixed with the carrot juice and orange zest, instead of blending the toasted spices, garlic, and ginger.

DO I REALLY HAVE TO REMIND YOU THAT SPINACH IS GOOD FOR YOU? IT TASTES SO GOOD YOU WOULD EAT IT ANYWAY.

FILET MIGNON WITH CRISP BACON, SEARED POLENTA, AND WILTED SPINACH SALAD

SERVES 4 /// PREP TIME: 20 MINUTES /// COOK TIME: 12 MINUTES

4 filet mignon steaks, about 4oz (115g) each, trimmed
2 tbsp tamari
Freshly ground black pepper
8 slices of "uncured" applewood-smoked bacon,
    each cut in thirds
1 red onion, finely chopped
1 garlic clove, thinly sliced
4 golden tomatoes, halved
4 vine-ripe tomatoes, halved
3 tbsp Muscat or Chardonnay wine vinegar
2 tbsp chopped fresh thyme
Finely grated zest of 1 lemon
9oz (250g) baby spinach leaves
18oz (500g) package ready-made plain polenta,
    cut in 8 slices
A little olive oil
2 tbsp chopped fresh flat-leaf (Italian) parsley leaves

> Season the steaks with the tamari and ground pepper, and let marinate while you prepare the rest of the dish. Preheat the broiler.

> Fry the bacon in a wok until crisp, about 5 minutes. Remove from the wok, drain on paper towels, and keep warm.

> Add the onion and garlic to the bacon fat and sauté, stirring, until softened and just turning lightly golden, about 2 minutes. Add the tomatoes and cook until softening but still holding their shape, about 3 minutes. Add the vinegar and bubble for a few seconds until almost evaporated. Add the thyme, lemon zest, and spinach. Season to taste. Stir gently until the spinach wilts, about 2 minutes. Remove from the heat.

> While the vegetable mixture is cooking, brush the polenta slices and steaks with a little olive oil and place them on the broiler rack about

5in (12.5cm) from the heat. Broil the polenta slices until they are golden brown, about 3–4 minutes on each side. Broil the steaks to the desired degree of doneness (2–6 minutes on each side).

> Reheat the wilted spinach. Transfer the steaks and polenta to warm plates and spoon the bacon, wilted spinach, and tomatoes alongside. Sprinkle with the parsley and serve.

BALSAMIC-FIG PORK CHOPS WITH BLUE CHEESE MASHED POTATOES

SERVES 4 /// PREP TIME: 25 MINUTES /// COOK TIME: 15–20 MINUTES

4 fresh rosemary sprigs

4 boneless pork chops, about
  6oz (175g) each

4 slices of "uncured" smoked bacon

1 tsp Southwestern Spice Rub
  (see page 63)

A little vegetable oil

4 tbsp balsamic-fig vinegar
  (or ordinary aged balsamic)

A few fresh rosemary sprigs
  for garnish

FOR THE POTATOES

1 ½ lb (675g) Yukon Gold (or other
  all-purpose potatoes), peeled and
  quartered lengthwise

2 tbsp crumbled blue cheese

2 tbsp sour cream or crème fraîche

1 tbsp butter

1 tbsp milk

2 tbsp snipped fresh chives

Kosher salt and freshly ground
  black pepper

> Place a sprig of rosemary in the center of each chop, then wrap a bacon slice around it. Season with the spice rub. Keep refrigerated until needed.

> Heat a ridged cast-iron grill pan. When hot, brush it with oil and add the pork chops, rosemary-side down. Cook for 10 minutes, turning the heat down to medium after the first 2 minutes. Turn the chops over and cook for another 10 minutes. Drizzle the balsamic vinegar over the chops. Turn the heat down to low and finish cooking, 5–10 minutes longer.

> While the chops are cooking, boil the potatoes in lightly salted water until tender, 15–20 minutes. Drain, reserving the cooking water, and return to the pan. Use a potato masher to mash the potatoes with the cheese, cream, butter, and milk. Add the snipped chives and beat with a wooden spoon or electric mixer just until smooth and fluffy. Season to taste.

> When the chops are cooked, transfer to plates and keep warm. Pour enough potato cooking water into the grill pan to cover the bottom. Bring to a boil, scraping up any meat residues. Taste the *jus* you've made and season, if necessary. Spoon the *jus* over the pork chops and spoon the potatoes alongside. Garnish with rosemary sprigs and serve.

LOBSTER SALAD WITH VANILLA VINAIGRETTE

SERVES 2 /// PREP TIME: 1 HOUR /// COOK TIME: 0

1 avocado

Fresh lemon juice

1–2 fresh palm hearts, peeled and
    sliced (or use canned)

1 tbsp extra virgin olive oil

1 good-sized cooked Maine lobster

4 moist, semi-dried tomatoes

1/2 tsp minced garlic

1 tsp chopped fresh thyme

1 mango, peeled, pitted, and
    finely diced

2 small handfuls of baby salad leaves

FOR THE VANILLA VINAIGRETTE

Juice of 1 orange, strained

1/4 vanilla bean

1 tsp wild-blossom honey

2 tbsp extra virgin olive oil

2 tbsp vegetable oil

Fresh lemon juice, strained

Kosher salt and white pepper

> First make the dressing. Put the orange juice in a small bowl. Split the vanilla bean and scrape the seeds into the bowl (discard the pod). Add the honey, then gradually whisk in the olive oil followed by the vegetable oil. Add lemon juice, salt, and pepper to taste.

> Peel, pit, and finely dice the avocado. Toss with a squeeze of lemon juice, to prevent browning. Season the palm hearts with 1 tsp lemon juice, a little salt and pepper, and the olive oil.

> Split the lobster in half. Remove the black vein that runs down the length of the body and lift out the tail meat. Cut in neat dice. Carefully remove the meat in one piece from each large claw.

> Stand a 2in (5cm) tall cylinder mold that is 2 1/2in (6cm) wide on a large serving plate. Arrange half the palm heart slices in the mold. Top with 2 tomatoes, pressing down slightly with a spoon. Lightly smear with garlic and sprinkle with thyme. Gently top with about one-third of the diced avocado, then one-third of the mango, and then add half the diced lobster tail, arranged attractively. Press down very gently with your fingers. Carefully lift off the mold. Repeat with a second plate.

> Whisk the vinaigrette again to combine, then spoon about 1 tbsp over each tower. Garnish the plates with the remaining diced avocado and mango. Gently place a shelled lobster claw against each tower. Lightly drizzle additional vinaigrette around the plates and garnish the towers with a few baby salad leaves.

// You can use 4 artichoke hearts (cooked or canned) instead of palm hearts, and shrimp instead of lobster, garnishing with cooked large shrimp.

STEAMED DUO OF SOLE AND HALIBUT WITH RAINBOW PEPPER STIR-FRY

SERVES 2 /// PREP TIME: 40 MINUTES /// COOK TIME: 7 MINUTES

2 small sole fillets (or 1 large sole or flounder fillet, halved lengthwise)
2 pinches of ground cumin
4oz (115g) piece of boneless halibut (or any meaty white fish), cut in half
2 fresh mint leaves
2 fresh chive stems
2 tsp rice vinegar
2 tsp tamari
1 tsp black sesame seeds
A few fresh chive stems for garnish

FOR THE STIR-FRY

2 tbsp sunflower or vegetable oil
4 green onions (scallions), cut in short lengths on the bias
1 red bell pepper, cut in thin strips
1 yellow bell pepper, cut in thin strips
2 cups pea shoots
1 fresh, hot, red chili, such as a Thai chili, seeded and chopped
12oz (350g) fresh egg noodles or cooked soba noodles
1 tsp cumin seeds
1 tsp caraway seeds
½in (1cm) piece of fresh ginger root, grated
1 garlic clove, very thinly sliced
2 tbsp tamari

> Lay the sole fillets, membrane-side up, on a board. Season each fillet with a pinch of cumin, then place a halibut portion in the center. Lay the mint on the halibut, then wrap the sole fillet around the halibut. Tie up each package with a chive stem (be gentle so the chive doesn't break).

> Place the packages in a bamboo steaming basket, or other steamer, lined with parchment paper. Season the fish with the rice vinegar and tamari, and sprinkle with the sesame seeds. Steam for 7 minutes.

> Meanwhile, heat the oil in a wok and stir-fry the onions, bell peppers, pea shoots, and chili for 3 minutes. Add the noodles, spices, ginger, garlic, and tamari, and stir-fry for 2 minutes longer.

> Spoon the stir-fry onto plates and arrange the fish alongside. Garnish with a few chive stems and serve.

TOFU WITH SPINACH AND CHILIES

SERVES 4 /// PREP TIME: 5 MINUTES /// COOK TIME: ABOUT 10 MINUTES

2 tbsp ghee or butter
1 small onion, chopped
1 tsp minced garlic
1 1/2 tsp minced fresh ginger root
1 tsp turmeric
1/2 tsp cumin seeds
1 tsp black mustard seeds
1 1/2 cups tomato purée
1–2 fresh jalapeño chilies, seeded and finely chopped
1 lb (450g) firm tofu, drained and diced
4 handfuls of baby spinach leaves
Freshly ground black pepper
1 lime, cut in wedges

> Heat the ghee or butter in a pan and sauté the onion with the garlic and ginger, stirring, until softened and fragrant, about 2 minutes. Add the turmeric, cumin seeds, and mustard seeds. When the mustard seeds begin to pop, add the tomato purée and chilies, and gently stir in the tofu. Bring to a boil. Reduce the heat and simmer very gently for 5 minutes.

> Add the spinach, cover, and cook gently until slightly wilted, 2–3 minutes longer. Season with pepper. Spoon into bowls, squeeze lime juice over, and serve with brown rice.

TORTELLONI WITH CREAMY FAVA BEANS AND THYME

SERVES 3–4 /// PREP TIME: 10 MINUTES /// COOK TIME: 8 MINUTES

1 ½ cups shelled fresh fava beans (or frozen baby lima beans, thawed)
1 ¼ cups strong chicken stock
3 tbsp cooked long grain rice
½ cup freshly grated Parmesan, plus extra for serving
1 large garlic clove, thinly sliced
2 tbsp chopped fresh thyme leaves
Freshly grated nutmeg
Kosher salt and freshly ground black pepper
12oz (350g) fresh tortelloni stuffed with cheese and ham
2 tbsp crème fraîche or heavy cream
2 tsp butter

> Blanch the fava beans in boiling water for 3 minutes. Drain and rinse with cold water, then slip the beans out of their skins.

> Put the stock, 1 cup of the fava beans, and the rice in a pan. Bring to a boil and boil for 5 minutes, stirring occasionally. Purée in a blender with the cheese, garlic, and thyme until smooth. Return to the pan. Season to taste with nutmeg, salt, and pepper.

> Cook the tortelloni according to package directions. Drain.

> Add the cream, butter, and remaining beans to the puréed bean sauce and heat through. Add the tortelloni and toss gently to coat. Serve with extra grated Parmesan.

// If you don't have any cooked rice, use a small potato, peeled and grated. After puréeing, this pasta sauce can be frozen in ice cube trays, for later use. Add the finishing touches when you thaw and reheat it.

SPANISH RICE

SERVES 4 /// PREP TIME: 5 MINUTES /// COOK TIME: 20 MINUTES

2 tbsp grapeseed oil
1 yellow onion, chopped
1 garlic clove, crushed
1 1/2 tsp mild chili powder
1 tsp ground cumin
1 1/2 tsp chopped jalapeño chilies (from a can or jar)
1 1/2 cups long grain rice
1 cup dry white wine
14oz (400g) can crushed tomatoes
2 cups boiling chicken stock
Kosher salt and freshly ground black pepper
2 tbsp chopped fresh thyme leaves

> Heat the oil in a pan and sauté the onion gently, stirring, until softened but not browned, about 2 minutes. Add the garlic, spices, and chilies, and cook, stirring, for 1 minute longer.

> Stir in the rice until it is glistening, then add the white wine. Boil rapidly until the wine has been absorbed. Add the tomatoes and simmer until the tomato juices are almost all gone, about 2 minutes.

> Stir in the stock. Bring back to a boil, then reduce the heat, cover, and simmer gently until the liquid is absorbed and the rice is tender, about 15 minutes. Season to taste, and stir in half the thyme. Garnish with the remaining thyme and serve hot.

// Serve this with pan-grilled large shrimp, salmon, tuna, or chicken.

WILD SALMON AND WARM BEET SALAD

SERVES 4 /// PREP TIME: 15 MINUTES /// COOK TIME: 30 MINUTES

1 bunch of red beets, greens and stems on
5 tbsp olive oil
2 yellow bell peppers, cut in chunks
4 slices "uncured" applewood-smoked bacon, diced
1 bunch of green onions (scallions), sliced
2–4 garlic cloves, thinly sliced
Kosher salt and freshly ground black pepper
4 thick pieces of wild salmon fillet, about 5oz (140g) each
A few grains of *fleur de sel* (French sea salt)
Juice of 2 oranges
About 4 tsp aged balsamic vinegar

> Remove the greens and stems from the beets, wash well, chop, and reserve. Peel the beets and cut in chunks. Heat 2 tbsp of the oil in a large, heavy-based skillet. Add the beets to one side of the pan, the bell peppers to the other. Cover and pan-roast over medium heat, turning once or twice, until tender, about 30 minutes.

> Meanwhile, heat 2 tbsp of the remaining oil in a wok. Add the bacon and sauté until golden, about 2 minutes. Add the green onions and garlic, and sauté for 1 minute longer. Add the chopped beet stems and greens. Stir-fry until wilted but still with some "bite," about 5 minutes. Season to taste. Remove from the wok with a draining spoon and set aside.

> Season the pieces of salmon fillet with *fleur de sel* and pepper. Heat the remaining oil in the wok. Sear the salmon, skin-side down, until crisp and golden, about 3 minutes. Turn the fillets over, add the orange juice, and cook for 3 minutes longer.

> Add the wilted greens to the cooked beets and bell peppers, and toss gently to heat through. Transfer to warm plates. Place the salmon fillets on top and spoon any pan juices over. Drizzle aged balsamic vinegar over each portion and serve.

FARFALLE WITH TUNA, WILTED SPINACH, SUN-DRIED TOMATOES, AND PINE NUTS

SERVES 4 /// PREP TIME: 5 MINUTES /// COOK TIME: 14–16 MINUTES

12oz (350g) farfalle (bowtie) pasta
2 tbsp olive oil
1 garlic clove, crushed
2 tsp harissa paste
12oz (350g) tuna loin, cubed
12oz (350g) baby spinach leaves
4 sun-dried tomatoes in olive oil, drained and chopped
12 cherry tomatoes, halved
1/2 cup chicken stock
1/3 cup sliced black olives
Kosher salt and freshly ground black pepper
Juice of 1/2 lemon
1/2 cup toasted pine nuts

> Cook the pasta in plenty of boiling salted water for about 10 minutes, or according to package directions. Drain and toss with 1 tbsp of the olive oil.

> While the pasta is cooking, heat the remaining olive oil in a large skillet. Add the garlic and harissa, and stir for a moment until they are fragrant. Add the tuna and sauté for 1–2 minutes. Add the spinach and move it around with tongs until it begins to wilt. Stir in the sun-dried tomatoes, cherry tomatoes, chicken stock, and olives. Bring to a boil and simmer until the cherry tomatoes have softened but are still holding their shape, about 2 minutes. Season with salt and pepper and sharpen with lemon juice.

> Stir in the pasta and toss well. Pile into warm, shallow pasta bowls and garnish with the pine nuts.

FATTOUSH

SERVES 4 /// PREP TIME: 25 MINUTES /// COOK TIME: 0

2 Roma or plum tomatoes, seeded and diced
2 green onions (scallions), thinly sliced
1 yellow bell pepper, diced
1 English cucumber, peeled and diced
¼ small red onion, chopped
A handful of fresh mint leaves, roughly chopped
A handful of fresh flat-leaf (Italian) parsley leaves, coarsely chopped
2 cups trimmed watercress or arugula, tightly packed
½ cup cubed feta cheese
½ cup pitted Kalamata olives

FOR THE PITA TOASTS
2 pita breads, split in half lengthwise
2 tsp extra virgin olive oil
1 ½ tsp *za'atar* (or ½ tsp each dried thyme, ground sumac,
   and sesame seeds, mixed together)

FOR THE DRESSING
¼ cup extra virgin olive oil
2 tbsp fresh lemon juice
1 small garlic clove, crushed
Kosher salt and freshly ground black pepper

> Preheat the oven to 350°F (180°C). Brush one side of the pita bread halves with olive oil and sprinkle with 1 tsp of the *za'atar*. Toast in the oven until the pitas are crisp and pale golden, 10–12 minutes. Set aside to cool.

> Whisk the dressing ingredients together in a large mixing bowl. Season to taste. Add the tomatoes, green onions, bell pepper, cucumber, red onion, mint, parsley, watercress or arugula, cheese, and olives to the bowl. Toss to coat everything evenly.

> Break the pitas into rough bite-size pieces and add them to the salad. Sprinkle with the remaining *za'atar*, and toss again. Taste and season with more salt, pepper, and lemon juice, if necessary. Serve immediately.

SEITAN OR QUORN CABBAGE SUSHI

MAKES 36 PIECES /// PREP TIME: 45 MINUTES /// COOK TIME: 25 MINUTES

6 large Savoy cabbage leaves

1 small eggplant

2oz (60g) seitan or Quorn, drained and minced

Scant 1 cup coconut milk

2 tbsp chopped fresh basil

2 tsp Thai green curry paste

1oz (30g) rice noodles

4 shiitake mushrooms, sliced

Juice of ½ lime

1½ tsp rice vinegar

2 tsp palm sugar or unrefined light brown sugar

1 small bunch of fresh mint

1 small carrot, shredded

A handful of pea shoots

2 tsp black onion or sesame seeds

Tamari for serving

> Blanch the cabbage leaves in about 1in (2.5cm) boiling water for 3 minutes. Drain, reserving the water. Rinse the leaves with cold water, then pat dry with paper towels. Remove the large rib toward the bottom of each leaf. Refrigerate the leaves until needed.

> Cook the whole eggplant in the cabbage water, covered, until tender when a knife is inserted through it, 15–20 minutes. Drain, rinse with cold water, and let cool.

> Simmer the seitan or Quorn in the coconut milk, stirring frequently, until thickened, about 5 minutes. Remove from the heat and stir in the basil and curry paste. Peel the eggplant, chop, and stir into the seitan mixture. Spread out on a plate to cool, then refrigerate.

> Cook the noodles for a minute or so longer than recommended on the package, so they are slightly sticky. Drain and let cool, then refrigerate.

> Mix the mushrooms with the lime juice, rice vinegar, and sugar. Refrigerate.

> When ready to assemble, lay a sheet of plastic wrap on a clean work surface. Cover with a bamboo rolling mat and lay another sheet of plastic wrap on this. Put a cabbage leaf on top, gently easing the two points together where the rib was cut out. Lay two or three mint leaves on the cabbage and then one-sixth of the sticky noodles. Spread one-sixth of the eggplant

mixture over the noodles, then add some of the carrot, then marinated mushrooms, and then a few pea shoots. Using the bamboo mat, roll up tightly, taking care not to roll the plastic wrap inside the cabbage roll. Wrap the roll in the plastic wrap and chill. Repeat with the remaining ingredients to make six long rolls in all.

> When ready to serve, trim the ends off the rolls and cut each one into six pieces. Arrange the sushi on plates. Sprinkle each piece with a few black onion or sesame seeds and a few drops of tamari.

// This also makes a stylish light lunch. If you don't have a rolling mat, use a sheet of heavy-duty foil.

TOFU NIÇOISE

SERVES 4 /// PREP TIME: 25 MINUTES /// COOK TIME: 0
3 tbsp extra virgin olive oil
Juice of $\frac{1}{2}$ lemon
$\frac{1}{2}$ tsp Dijon mustard
1 garlic clove, crushed
1 small zucchini, sliced
$\frac{1}{2}$ small red onion, thinly sliced
4oz (115g) thin green beans, trimmed, steamed until tender, and drained
4oz (115g) sun-dried tomatoes in oil, drained and halved
$\frac{1}{3}$ cup pitted Niçoise olives
2 tsp capers
4 fresh flat-leaf (Italian) parsley sprigs, chopped
1lb (450g) firm tofu, drained and cubed
Kosher salt and freshly ground black pepper

> Whisk together the olive oil, lemon juice, mustard, and garlic in a medium bowl. Add the zucchini, red onion, beans, tomatoes, olives, capers, and half the parsley, tossing to coat everything well.

> Add the tofu and toss gently, being careful not to break it up. Season with salt and pepper to taste. Serve garnished with the remaining parsley.

THAI FORBIDDEN RICE SALAD

SERVES 4 /// PREP TIME: 10 MINUTES /// COOK TIME: 30 MINUTES

1 cup Thai black rice (also called forbidden rice)
Kosher salt and freshly ground black pepper
2 tbsp tamari
2 tsp toasted sesame oil
Juice of 1/2 lime
1/2 tsp *sambal oelek* or hot chili paste
1 cup roasted, unsalted cashews
1/2 red bell pepper, finely chopped
1/2 yellow bell pepper, finely chopped
6 green onions (scallions), thinly sliced

> Put the rice, 2 cups water, and a pinch of salt in a pan. Bring to a boil, then cover, reduce the heat, and simmer gently until the liquid is absorbed and the rice is tender, about 30 minutes.

> Meanwhile, whisk the tamari, sesame oil, lime juice, and *sambal oelek* or chili paste together in a salad bowl. Add the cashews, red and yellow bell peppers, and green onions.

> When the rice is ready, add it to the mixture and toss to coat everything well. Add salt, pepper, and additional *sambal oelek* or lime juice to taste. Serve warm or at room temperature.

// If you can't get Thai black rice, try wild rice, or wild rice mixed with long grain rice, instead and cook according to package directions.

PICK ME UP

IN THE WORKING DAY, YOU NEED REGULAR PITSTOPS TO UP YOUR FUEL INTAKE. SNACKS AND GRAB-AND-GO WRAPS SHOULD BE SIMPLE, MESS-FREE COMBINATIONS THAT BUILD UP AN EXCITING FLAVOR PROFILE WITH CONTRASTING TEXTURES AND TASTES. AVOID MESSY, DRIPPY FOOD AND YOU WON'T BE WIPING IT OFF YOUR KEYBOARD OR YOUR DESK.

BANANA-PEANUT BUTTER WRAP—GREEN TEA

SERVES 1 /// PREP TIME: 5 MINUTES /// COOK TIME: 0
1 soft whole wheat or corn tortilla
2 tbsp smooth peanut butter
2 tbsp orange-blossom honey
1 banana
A squeeze of lemon juice
A cup of strong-brewed green tea

> Lay the tortilla on a sheet of wax paper. Spread with the peanut butter
and then the honey. Thinly slice the banana and toss with the lemon juice
to prevent browning (particularly if you aren't going to eat this right
away). Fold the tortilla in half and half again to make a triangular cone,
then fill with the sliced banana. Enjoy with a cup of green tea.

TAKE THIS ONE TO WORK.

DRIED MANGO—JERKY—SUNFLOWER SEEDS

SERVES UP TO 4 /// PREP TIME: 2 MINUTES /// COOK TIME: 0

6oz (175g) package all-natural beef jerky
4oz (115g) dried mango
8oz (225g) unsalted toasted sunflower seeds

> Eat the above ingredients together for a quick midmorning snack.

// You can exchange ingredients to fit your lifestyle—try dried cranberries and pumpkin seeds with turkey jerky for a change.

GRAB & GO

SUNFLOWER SEEDS ARE AN EXCELLENT SOURCE OF "HAPPY-MAKING" B VITAMINS.

APPLE—YOGURT—ALMONDS

SERVES 1 /// PREP TIME: 3 MINUTES /// COOK TIME: 0
1 apple, sliced
1 cup vanilla yogurt
6oz (175g) toasted almonds

> Just simply eat until full. Save what you haven't finished for later.

GORGONZOLA AND WALNUT CROSTINI

SERVES 1 /// PREP TIME: 2 MINUTES /// COOK TIME: 6–7 MINUTES
1–2 thick slices of whole wheat walnut bread
2–4 tsp wild-blossom honey
1–2oz (30–60g) creamy Gorgonzola cheese
A few edible flowers

> Preheat the broiler. Lightly toast the bread on both sides under the broiler. Spread the toast with the honey and then with the cheese. Broil until the cheese melts and is just turning golden around the edges, 2–3 minutes. Garnish with a few edible flowers and eat.

DRIED CHERRY CHUTNEY WITH GOAT CHEESE AND CRACKERS

MAKES 1 JAR /// PREP TIME: 5 MINUTES /// COOK TIME: 10 MINUTES

1 cup dried cherries
1/3 cup unrefined light brown sugar
1/3 cup sherry vinegar
2 tbsp finely chopped candied ginger
4 tbsp apple cider
2 tbsp fresh lemon juice
1/2 tsp dried chili flakes
Pinch of ground cardamom

FOR SERVING
Goat cheese, wholegrain crackers, and tender young celery ribs

> Put all the ingredients in a small, heavy-based pan. Bring to a boil, then reduce the heat and simmer over medium heat until thickened, about 10 minutes. Pot, cool, and label. Store in the refrigerator (the chutney will keep for several weeks).

> To serve, slice cylinders of goat cheese, using a wet knife, and arrange on plates with some wholegrain crackers and celery. Add a heaped spoonful of the chutney to each plate.

// This chutney is also great with cold meats and curries.

SMOKED SALMON—SUN-DRIED CRANBERRIES—GOAT CHEESE WRAP

SERVES 1 /// PREP TIME: 6 MINUTES /// COOK TIME: 0

1 soft whole wheat tortilla

About 1oz (30g) goat cheese

2 slices of smoked wild salmon

1 tbsp sun-dried cranberries

A handful of bean sprouts or daikon sprouts

> Lay a sheet of wax paper on a board. Put the tortilla on top. Spread the goat cheese across the tortilla, followed by the smoked salmon. Strew the sun-dried cranberries over and, finally, top with the sprouts.

> Looking at the tortilla as if it were a clock, begin to roll from six o'clock and continue all the way around to make a cone. Secure in the paper.

GOOD SNACKS KEEP YOU FROM EATING JUNK, AND HELP PREVENT YOU FROM OVEREATING AT THE NEXT MEALTIME.

SPINACH LATKES

MAKES 12 /// PREP TIME: 15 MINUTES /// COOK TIME: 6–8 MINUTES

3 potatoes (preferably russet), about 1lb (450g) in total, peeled
1 cup chopped fresh wilted spinach (or thawed frozen spinach)
1 small onion, grated
3 tbsp matzo meal or unbleached all-purpose flour
Kosher salt and freshly ground black pepper
2 eggs, beaten
Vegetable or grapeseed oil

> Grate the potatoes into a bowl. Squeeze the potatoes to drain off excess moisture. Squeeze out the moisture from the spinach. Drain the onion. Mix all the vegetables together and stir in the matzo meal or flour, some seasoning, and the eggs.

> Pour enough oil into a skillet to coat the bottom and heat over medium heat. Put three spoonfuls of the mixture in the pan, spaced well apart, and press out to make cakes about 4in (10cm) diameter. Cook until golden brown, about 3–4 minutes on each side. Keep the latkes warm in a low oven while cooking the remainder.

> Serve with a fresh herb salad dressed with vinaigrette.

I CAME UP WITH THESE FOR HANUKKAH, WHICH WAS THE FIRST HOLIDAY WE EVER CELEBRATED AT GOOGLE.

WATERMELON SATÉ WITH HONEY-VINEGAR DIPPING SAUCE

SERVES UP TO 8 /// PREP TIME: 10 MINUTES /// COOK TIME: 2 MINUTES

6 tbsp orange-blossom honey
4 tbsp sherry vinegar
¼ tsp ground cinnamon
¼ tsp habanero chili powder
¼ tsp kosher salt
1 small watermelon

> First prepare the sauce. Put the honey, vinegar, cinnamon, chili powder, salt, and 1 tbsp water in a small saucepan and bring to a boil, stirring. Remove from the heat and pour into a small dish. Let cool, then chill.

> Cut wedges from the melon (as much as you like). Peel them and remove the seeds, if desired, then cut in chunks. Thread the chunks onto small wooden skewers.

> When you are ready to serve this amazingly refreshing snack, just platter up as many of the melon skewers as you need, place the dipping sauce on the platter, and go out and make some people happy.

// You get the five S's with this dish: sweet, sour, salty, spicy, and slightly savory—not exactly umami! If you're not sharing with friends, you probably won't eat a whole watermelon at once, but make all the dipping sauce. Store it in the refrigerator and then you can make more saté sticks whenever you fancy a snack.

SWEET POTATO BISCUITS

MAKES ABOUT 15 /// PREP TIME: 30 MINUTES /// COOK TIME: 15 MINUTES

1 small sweet potato, cut in small chunks
2 cups unbleached all-purpose flour
1 tbsp baking powder
½ tsp baking soda
½ tsp ground cinnamon
½ tsp fine sea salt
4 tbsp (½ stick) cold unsalted butter, cut in 6 pieces
1 cup buttermilk
2 tbsp wild-blossom honey

> Cook the sweet potato in boiling water until soft, about 6 minutes.
Drain and mash well. You need about ½ cup.

> Preheat the oven to 425°F (220°C). Line a baking sheet with a silicone
baking mat or parchment paper.

> Sift the flour, baking powder, baking soda, cinnamon, and salt into a
bowl. Cut the butter into the flour mixture with two knives or a pastry
blender (or use your cool fingertips to rub it in) until the mixture
resembles coarse crumbs.

> In a separate bowl, mix the buttermilk, mashed sweet potato, and
honey. Mix the potato mixture into the flour mixture until just combined.

> Turn the mixture onto a floured board and knead gently, one or two
times, just to bring the dough together. Press out into a round about
½in (1cm) thick. Cut out biscuits using a 3in (7.5cm) round cutter or
glass. Knead the trimmings and cut out more biscuits.

> Arrange a little apart on the baking sheet. Bake until the biscuits are
golden, about 15 minutes. Remove to a rack to cool slightly. Serve warm
or at room temperature, split open, with butter and honey.

SMOKED SALMON TARTLETS

MAKES 12 /// PREP TIME: 20 MINUTES /// COOK TIME: 8–10 MINUTES

6 large, rectangular sheets of phyllo pastry
1–2 tbsp sunflower oil
7oz (200g) Neufchâtel or cream cheese
1 tbsp milk
2 tbsp snipped fresh chives
2 tsp fresh lemon juice
4oz (115g) smoked wild salmon trimmings or slices, chopped
Kosher salt and freshly ground black pepper
2oz (60g) salmon caviar

> Preheat the oven to 375°F (190°C). Brush a sheet of phyllo pastry with a little oil and fold in half. Brush with a little oil again. Cut in half to form two oblongs. Fold these in half to form squares. Brush with oil again. Repeat with the remaining sheets of phyllo. Press the squares into 12 lightly oiled individual tart pans. Bake until crisp and golden, 8–10 minutes. Let cool.

> Beat the cheese with the milk, chives, and lemon juice. Separate the pieces of salmon and mix in. Season the mixture to taste.

> When ready to serve, spoon the salmon mixture into the phyllo cases and garnish each with a small spoonful of salmon caviar.

MINT-CHOCOLATE BROWNIES

MAKES 16 /// PREP TIME: 30 MINUTES /// COOK TIME: ABOUT 35 MINUTES

12 tbsp (1½ sticks) unsalted butter
6oz (175g) bittersweet chocolate
1½ cups unbleached all-purpose flour
2 tbsp unsweetened cocoa powder
½ tsp fine sea salt
4 eggs
2 cups unrefined granulated sugar
1 tsp peppermint extract
1 tsp pure vanilla extract
2 cups bittersweet or semisweet chocolate chips

> Preheat the oven to 350°F (180°C). Butter an 8in (20cm) square baking pan and set aside.

> Melt the butter and chocolate together in a double boiler or in a bowl set over, but not touching, simmering water in a pan. Stir until smooth. Remove from the heat and let cool.

> Sift the flour, cocoa powder, and salt into a small bowl. Beat the eggs and sugar together with an electric mixer until very thick and pale, and the beaters leave a trail when lifted out of the mixture. Mix in the melted chocolate and the peppermint and vanilla extracts at lowest speed. Fold in the flour mixture and the chocolate chips, mixing just until the batter is no longer streaky.

> Transfer the batter to the prepared pan. Bake until a toothpick inserted about 1in (2.5cm) from the edge comes out clean, about 35 minutes. The top should feel set, but the center should still be quite soft. (If the toothpick comes out very wet, test another place to be sure you didn't poke into a melted chocolate chip.) Transfer the pan to a rack to cool and cut into squares when cold. Store the brownies in an airtight container.

COCONUT-OATMEAL BARS WITH CHOCOLATE CHIPS

MAKES 16 /// PREP TIME: 15 MINUTES /// COOK TIME: 25 MINUTES

½ cup unbleached all-purpose flour
¼ tsp baking powder
¼ tsp fine sea salt
1 cup rolled oats
½ cup unrefined light brown sugar, lightly packed
½ cup dried, unsweetened, shredded coconut
½ cup bittersweet or semisweet chocolate chips
6 tbsp unsalted butter, melted and cooled to room temperature
1 large egg, lightly beaten
¼ tsp natural vanilla extract

> Preheat the oven to 350°F (180°C). Lightly oil an 8in (20cm) square baking pan and set aside.

> Sift the flour, baking powder, and salt into a mixing bowl. Stir in the oats, brown sugar, coconut, and chocolate chips. Stir together the melted butter, egg, and vanilla, then add to the flour mixture and stir just until blended. Avoid mixing more than needed. Transfer to the prepared pan and level the surface.

> Bake until slightly risen, golden, and just firm to the touch, about 25 minutes. Put the pan on a rack and let cool before cutting into triangular or rectangular bars or squares.

PACK THESE IN YOUR BAG AND EAT THEM ON THE WAY TO WORK.

GOOGLE HOT SAUCE

MAKES 1 JAR /// PREP TIME: 15 MINUTES /// COOK TIME: 45 MINUTES

1 cup fresh habanero chilies, roughly chopped
1/3 cup fresh jalapeño chilies, roughly chopped
1 dried chipotle chili, crushed
2 tbsp tomato paste
1 tbsp minced ginger
1 tbsp tamarind paste
1 tbsp pomegranate molasses
1 1/2 tbsp apple cider vinegar
1/3 cup fresh orange juice
4 tsp unrefined light brown sugar
Juice of 1 lime
1 small carrot, finely diced
1 small onion, finely chopped
1 celery rib, finely chopped
2 tbsp Worcestershire sauce
1 tbsp Thai fish sauce
3 tbsp good drinking red wine

> Place all the ingredients in a heavy-based pan. Add ½ cup water. Bring to a boil, then reduce the heat, cover the pan, and simmer very gently, stirring occasionally, until rich and thick and the vegetables are very soft, about 45 minutes.

> Purée in a blender, then pass through a strainer. Add a little more water to thin to the desired consistency. Store in a clean, sealed jar in the refrigerator. Serve to fire up any of the recipes that call for chili sauce, or use on tacos, crostini, wraps, or even peanut butter sandwiches!

INDEX

SOURCES

//
> Sriracha Hot Chili Sauce is made by Huy Fong Foods, Inc. in Rosemead, California. You can find it at most Asian markets and even some mainstream supermarket chains (www.huyfong.com).
//
> The Three Crabs brand of fish sauce is available in most Asian markets, distributed in the United States by Viet Huong Fish Sauce Co. in San Francisco.
//
> Kewpie, or QP, mayonnaise is available in most Asian markets and online.
//
> To find fennel pollen for cheese-flavored oil, try www.fennelpollen.com or www.thespicehouse.com
//
> Both kamut and farro, as well as other grains, are sold at Whole Foods markets.
//
> I find the Monterey Bay Aquarium's Seafood WATCH program to be an invaluable resource for helping me decide which fishes are okay to eat. Designed to raise consumer awareness about the importance of buying seafood from sustainable sources, the program has an outstanding Website that helps consumers across the United States learn which seafood to buy or avoid in their particular regions. Before you buy another piece of fish, go to: www.mbayaq.org/cr/seafoodwatch.asp. On the Website, you can even print pocket-sized guides to take to the store. I don't buy any seafood that doesn't meet the Monterey Bay Aquarium's sustainable fishing guidelines, and you shouldn't either.
//

THANK YOU

// To my wife and son for dealing with and putting up with me and all the late-night cooking, testing of recipes, endless hours of research, and photo shoots, and for allowing the media into our home on a moment's notice. Thank you Kimmie for all the love and support you show me in my many projects that often end up dragging you in as well.

// To my parents and brother for supporting me, even when we all thought this path I had decided to travel in life would never pay off. Thank you for having faith and believing in my abilities, and helping me to pursue my dreams of becoming a chef.

// To Larry Page and Sergey Brin for taking a leap of faith in bringing me in as Google's very first executive chef. Thank you for allowing me to grow with your company and be part of your world. Many times I felt like Homer Simpson around the two of you. Thank you George Salah for actually being the guy at Google to hire me, relating to me as well as you could, and for encouraging me to create a really special experience for the Googlers every day. Thank you Jim Glass and the Google Culinary Team for being such a great kick ass group of people—you know who you are.

// To the entire Google family—to everyone who ever had the courage to ring the bell when we weren't open yet, to all who ever volunteered to work in the café when I was shorthanded, and to those who contributed recipes they thought would be appreciated. (Were they surprised when I served them! Of course I tweaked them slightly.) And to all the extended Google family that would volunteer to help out with big celebration meals and events, Hanukkah, Chinese New Year, and Big Ass BBQs.

// To the Marin & Sonoma County Crew for believing in me and supporting me through the years. To all the chefs and restaurateurs I ever worked under who taught me what to do and what not to do. To all the vendors who have taken care of me over the years. Special thanks to Steve Kimock, Chef Cat Cora, Chef Ming Tsai, Chef Ken Orringer, David Vise, and Karen Alexander, for the kind words, great food, and amazing music. Thank you to the legal team at Wilson, Sonsini Goodrich & Rosati.

// To Nuba Bear of Three Captains Sea Products, Half Moon Bay, CA; Dee Harley of Harley Farms Goat Dairy, Pescadero, CA, Phipps Country Farm, Pescadero, CA; The Wild Butcher at Dittmer's Gourmet Meats and Wurst-Haus, Mountain View, CA; Sigona's Farmer's Market in Redwood City, CA; San Francisco Ferry Plaza Farmers' Market; Fairfax Farmer's Market, Fairfax, CA; Whole Foods Markets; Trader Joe's; Cowgirl Creamery; Bassian Farms; Sky Vodka; Anchor Steam Brewery; and Vegiworks.

// To the kind folks over at DK Publishing for giving me the opportunity to create this cookbook. To the creative team over at Smith & Gilmour in the UK, and to Noel Murphy Photography. Thanks to Alex and Noel for being able to hang with me for a couple of days in the States and drink some local beer.

// To all the artists and musicians in my life for allowing me to share in your world. Without you, life would be so boring.

// To Al Gore for caring about the planet. To Howard Cohen. To God for helping me get this done. Most importantly, Thank You for buying this book.

// A portion of the proceeds from this book will be donated to charity.